Promises Kept

➤ Sustaining
➤ School and District
➤ Leadership in a
➤ Turbulent Era

Steven Jay Gross

Foreword by Carl D. Glickman and Marla W. McGhee

 Association for Supervision and Curriculum Development ➤ Alexandria, Virginia ➤ USA

Association for Supervision and Curriculum Development
1703 N. Beauregard St. Alexandria, VA 22311-1714 USA
Phone: 800-933-2723 or 703-578-9600 Fax: 703-575-5400
Web site: http://www.ascd.org E-mail: member@ascd.org

Gene R. Carter, *Executive Director;* Nancy Modrak, *Director of Publishing;* Julie Houtz, *Director of Book Editing & Production;* Ernesto Yermoli, *Project Manager;* Georgia McDonald, *Senior Graphic Designer;* Jim Beals, *Typesetter;* Vivian Coss, *Production Specialist*

Paperback ISBN: 0-87120-973-X ASCD product #101078 List Price: $25.95 ($20.95 ASCD member price, direct from ASCD only)   s10/04

e-books ($25.95): netLibrary ISBN 1-4166-0148-1 ebrary ISBN 1-4166-0149-X

Library of Congress Cataloging-in-Publication Data
Gross, Steven J.
   Promises kept : sustaining school and district leadership in a turbulent era / Steven Jay Gross.
      p. Cm.
   Includes bibliographical references and index.
   ISBN 0-87120-973-X (alk. Paper)
   1. School management and organization. 2. Educational leadership. I. Title.

   LB2805.G77 2004
   371.2—dc22
                                        2004013558

10 09 08 07 06 05 04   12 11 10 9 8 7 6 5 4 3 2 1

Promises Kept

Sustaining School and District Leadership in a Turbulent Era

Foreword

STEVEN GROSS BEGINS THIS BOOK BY HOPING "THAT IT WILL HELP YOU DEAL with one of the most serious challenges we face in education: sustaining your school's progress in a time of serious disruption." School leaders— whether administrators, supervisors, or teachers—know exactly what he means by "serious disruption."

From year to year, leaders are bombarded with uncertain funding, faculty turnover, and unfunded mandates while continuing to focus on the absolutely correct mission of educating all students for a democratic society, regardless of social class, ethnic identity, native language, or special need. The unfortunate irony is that activities conducted in the name of this most important mission often have the reverse effect. Achievement measurements attached to high stakes accountability systems and state tests are pushing children, and adults, down and out. Educators in many successful schools are demoralized and frustrated as top down emphasis on more and more testing has pulled them away from comprehensive learning achievements and the hallmark of their practice—students demonstrating what they know through engagement, participation, and real world connections. And compounding these disruptions are confusing messages about what local communities, districts, and state and federal decision-makers actually desire. For example, government officials demand better test results, yet parents often want their own child to enjoy learning above everything else. Plus, all the scuffling and contending about needs of various constituents happens in the midst of hectic, day-to-day school-based activity. Recently, in a single day, we observed a school leader trying to take care of a student dozing off due to lack of sleep and inadequate health care, a broken down air conditioner, a central office query about overdue paperwork, an angry parent requesting immediate attention, and two of the most stalwart veteran teachers, who pioneered the original school redesign, announcing their intention to retire at year's end. This book shows how leaders in change-oriented schools have managed to work through disruptions to stay true to a vision of learning. The central thesis, based on a close examination of exemplary U.S. schools, is that when leaders understand that success is based on collecting, conveying, and supporting important education ideas rather than on status, power, or charisma, then change can be planned, implemented, and sustained despite disruptions. Moreover, the book shows how sustaining school success through different political and economic phases is a function both of change making and change management. Unlike most writing on school change, this book explains complex theory and practice in a thoughtful, elegantly written way. Steve Gross has provided us with an insightful and practical guide for navigating the swirls and eddies ahead. This book is replete with descriptions, strategies, easy-to-use charts, and specific examples. Case studies show how pioneer educators have helped build schools around compelling educational ideas to attract new generations that can build upon their achievements and create even more powerful education for students. Read this book alone or with faculty, staff, students, parents, district personnel, or school board members. Let it help you act on the immediate needs of students, and let it guide you in your role as steward of the present and future. We are grateful to Steve for writing this book. It is indeed a text for our time.

— *Carl D. Glickman and Marla W. McGhee*
Southwest Texas State University

Acknowledgments

THIS BOOK WAS A LONG TIME IN THE MAKING AND IS THE RESULT OF GREAT collegiality shown to me. I wish to thank the educators around the United States and Canada who opened themselves to me with such enthusiasm; I have done my best to portray the lessons learned clearly and accurately. I would also like to thank Carl Glickman and Marla McGhee for writing such a kind foreword. Carolyn Pool and Ernesto Yermoli of ASCD have spent many hours guiding me and helping me to polish my ideas, and I am in their debt. Finally, I would like to thank my family and my Temple University family, especially my colleague Joan Shapiro, for supporting these ideas when they were only fragile brainstorms. Your encouragement has meant more than you realize.

Preface

If you live to be a thousand, you can never learn it all. The art of sailing is as old as mankind and as new as the cat's paw you see scurry down from windward.

—H. A. Calahan (1932/1999, p. 3)

I WANT TO WELCOME YOU TO THE CONTINUATION OF AN ADVENTURE. THE journey started with my work in curriculum, instruction, and assessment as a teacher, district curriculum director, state chief of curriculum and instruction, and professor of educational leadership. Over the past 25 years I have seen and participated in many innovations, from the classroom to the state level. Working in public schools, higher education, the private sector, and state government, my partners and I have been able to carry fresh ideas from the design stage to implementation so often that invention became a wonderful habit.

I have seen many similar efforts at schools and districts across North America over the past eight years. In my 1998 book, *Staying Centered: Curriculum Leadership in a Turbulent Era,* I documented the work of 10 such schools. These were amazing places to study because they offered clear examples of educators working harder and smarter than I had ever seen, experimenting methodically, and measuring progress intelligently in the name of the students they served. Like the benevolent teachers they were, the educators in these schools showed great patience with me.

One day I visited a principal in a small school to get a better grasp of her curriculum work for multi-aged classes. I was very moved by the quality of her program, and told her that she had made wonderful progress.

"Steve," she said, "We are never going to get *there*. We will always be on the way."

Of course, I knew that this was true—that the processes of refinement and reinvention were built into the reform program by design. What impressed me was how clearheaded she was about the issue of constant development, and how enthusiastically she grasped the challenge.

In *Staying Centered,* I described four important steps that faculty at the schools I studied took to sustain curriculum leadership:

1. Initiating change;
2. Selecting a curriculum-instruction-assessment approach;
3. Establishing professional development practices; and
4. Handling challenges to their work, which I define as turbulence.

I covered approximately the first five years of curriculum leadership development at each of the schools discussed in the book, and their stories are very instructive for those who wish to begin the complex but inspiring process of deep reform. But life at these schools didn't stop after five years, and questions soon arose for which I had no answers. What happens when a powerful leader leaves? How can an innovating school keep its learning agenda alive? What do schools do to bring new teachers, students, and families into the community while at the same time keeping talented veterans inspired? Finally, what do reforming schools do when district, state, and federal upheavals threaten to turn their programs upside down? To answer these powerful questions, I went back into the field, traveling across the United States to visit old friends and new ones alike. If *Staying Centered* is the story of innovating schools making promising beginnings, this book is my attempt to find out how innovating schools followed through over the first decade and a half.

A Word About the Organization of This Book

One thing that has not changed over the years is the busy pace of educators at all levels. Much as we would like to sit and contemplate the issues before us, we seldom have time for deep reflection. The demands of our work mean that we are quite selective in our reading and usually want to see concrete benefits. Knowing this, I have designed this book to be used quickly and easily by teachers, administrators, board members, community members, and students of educational reform and innovation. Because many readers are likely to be strong spatial learners, I have included many diagrams and graphics to illustrate major ideas.

The book is divided into the following four sections:

- **Challenge 1** is intended to help you work through the steep challenge of leadership succession. Here you will explore possible patterns of leadership change, as well as ways to help new leaders get off to a successful start reforming their schools.
- **Challenge 2** focuses on keeping the learning agenda alive. Here you will see how schools deal with the pressures of rapid growth and increased demands on faculty, staff, and administration. I also discuss the pivotal role of shared governance in helping schools remember their missions and stay on course.
- **Challenge 3** explains how successful schools keep the culture of invention alive in the face of inevitable staff turnover. You will also discover how schools welcome new students and families by helping them understand the school culture, and how they learn from every new arrival.
- **Challenge 4** shows how leading schools deal with serious disruptions from the world beyond their walls. In this chapter you will find new ways to deal with changes at the district level, your state's accountability system, and the No Child Left Behind legislation. You will also learn how schools can recast their visions to fit new demands without selling out core values.

Readers with special interests may want to use this book as a direct follow-up to ideas found in *Staying Centered.* For this reason, I have written the chapters so that they align. If you have a particular concern, feel free to start with an issue in *Staying Centered* and follow it up with the corresponding section of this book.

Every section of this book begins with something I call a "turbulence gauge." Throughout the book, I have developed Turbulence Theory to describe the tossing and turning that schools face when working on their development. The purpose of the gauge is to help you determine how relevant the chapter is to your school right now. Take a minute to consider the turbulence gauge for Challenge 1 (see Figure C-1) to see what I mean. This particular turbulence gauge focuses on the issue of leadership succession. The "degrees of turbulence" in the left column reflect four general levels of volatility in schools. These levels are defined in the center column, and their relevance to the chapter topic is outlined in the right column.

The gauge is pretty straightforward. As you look at each challenge, consider only where your own school fits in the rubric. *You do not have to read this book in a linear way if you do not want to.* You may prefer to use the gauges at the start of each section to decide where to begin reading, and where to go from there. For example, if you are not dealing with a leadership succession problem this year, but *are* faced with a serious challenge from the state, it should be easy for you to determine that you should start with Challenge 4. Like a sailor trimming the sails on a four-mast ship, your goal is not to completely avoid turbulence but to adjust your situation so that you are not overwhelmed by it. You need to visualize the work ahead and prioritize your work carefully before moving on. Turbulence is inevitable—but like the wind filling the sails, it can be useful as well.

Most of the chapters follow the same format. First, I provide some background on the issue. Next, I provide suggestions on how to go from learning about an issue to gaining the confidence to respond. To help make the connection between the issue being discussed and your own needs, each challenge ends with specific steps to help you implement the suggestions in your own setting.

My fondest hope for this book is that it will help you deal with one of the most serious challenges we face in education: sustaining a school's progress in a time of serious disruption. By addressing crucial issues with practical examples and strategies, I hope that the book will do more than merely raise interesting questions—I want this book to serve as a compass, helping you navigate the turbulent waters ahead.

Challenge 1

All we know is that there was a glory and that it is no more; all we know is that for the moment there is darkness, not so dark certainly because when we look into our hearts we still find the living flame which he lighted there.

—Jawaharlal Nehru
(on the death of Mahatma Gandhi)

Dealing with Leadership Succession

FIGURE C-1
TURBULENCE GAUGE FOR CHALLENGE 1

Degree of Turbulence	General Definition	Relevant Scenario
Light	Associated with ongoing issues Little or no disruption to the normal work environment Subtle signs of stress	The highly regarded leader is so important to the reform effort that it seems nearly impossible for that person to leave without some disruption, especially in the early years of reform.
Moderate	Widespread awareness of the issue and its specific origins	The transition is not a surprise, and has been planned for through a lot of dialogue at many levels. People inside and beyond the school seem comfortable with the succession plan.
Severe	Possibility of large-scale community demonstrations A sense of crisis	The school has had surprise changes in leadership at awkward times. There is no agreed-upon plan in place to deal with succession, and people are nervous that the next leader may not understand or fully support the reform program.
Extreme	Structural damage to the school's reform Collapse of the reform seems likely	The leader is leaving in exasperation, and there is a sense that his departure marks the end of the reform program.

Challenge 1

When I speak to people about my interest in leadership succession, I often get a quizzical response. "Why is that such a fascinating topic?" people ask. "Isn't this issue just a little obscure?"

I understand the reaction. Preparing for changes in top leadership may be important, but it's not a high priority for most of us on a typical workday. Yet once every four years, when voting for president, we do deal with questions of leadership succession. We may rejoice in this process, bemoan its shortcomings, or joke about its frequent twists and turns, but the fact remains that we must consider where we would like the country to be and who we think can best lead us there. The peaceful transition of power from one leader to the next is an essential characteristic of democratic government and a vital measure of its success.

Educators seem to pay little attention to the question of transition, at least until they are faced with the imminent departure of a trusted principal or superintendent. This situation reminds me of a passage I once read in a book about family businesses that pass from one generation to the next. The author had convinced the aging founder of a company to craft a leadership succession strategy, but the CEO still betrayed his reluctance.

"You're right," he told the author. "I do need to think about what might happen *if* I should ever die."

Of course, succession is not a question of *if* but of *when*, and wise leadership teams need to consider it carefully and directly.

To help you accomplish this, we will consider three issues dealing with leadership succession. First, it is important to understand patterns and choices in the leadership succession process. Next, we will look at leadership mentoring—a powerful model for helping newly arrived leaders. Finally, we will expand the very concept of leadership and look at schools run by small teams of teachers who have become full-time administrators.

My goal is for you to develop a better understanding of leadership succession and discover one or more strategies that make sense in your setting as you start to take action. In this way, you will take the first crucial step needed to calm down the turbulence in your school and make further progress toward reform more likely.

Before reading any further, please use the Turbulence Gauge in Figure C-1 to see how relevant this section is to your current situation.

Understanding the Patterns of Leadership Succession

I OFTEN THINK ABOUT THE SCHOOL-REFORM LEADERS I WROTE ABOUT IN *Staying Centered*. While their situations differed, their behavior was remarkably similar, as was the effect that they had in the early days of their schools' development. The high degree of support the leaders enjoyed almost obscured the inevitable: that one day all of them were going to leave their beloved schools, and their districts would need to find new people to take the reform programs to the next level.

This obvious but painful truth led me to examine a cross section of reforming schools that had moved from the first to the second generation of leadership. Their stories help answer the questions: What directions can leaders take upon assuming office, and what patterns are there in the leadership cycle that can help us better understand the process?

Background

The question of leadership succession is ancient, appearing in the literature, lore, and sacred texts of many societies. There is, however, a more recent body of work to consult. Burns's *Leadership* (1978) is one particularly well-known text and helped introduce the idea of "transformational leadership," which aims to make fundamental structural changes in schools and districts. This issue has received serious attention over the past decade from such authors as Fullan and Stiegerbauer (1991),

4

Leithwood (1992), Lieberman (1995), and Sergiovanni (1996). Grusky's *Administrative Theory in Transition* (1960) provides a thoughtful overview of leadership succession in formal organizations. Gordon and Rosen's article "Critical Factors in Leadership Succession" (1981) divides succession into pre- and post-arrival stages, each containing its own separate issues. In "Leadership Succession in School Settings" (1985), Miskel and Cosgrove add a third stage to Gordon and Rosen's model.

Hoy and Aho's "Patterns of Succession in High School Principals and Organizational Change" (1973) examines the differences between principals promoted from within the school and those hired from outside, concluding that the latter are more likely to support innovation. Hart's "Succession as Social Validation: The View from Inside the Principalship" (1985) is an autobiographical case study of the author's experiences as the first female principal in her district, and emphasizes the importance of social factors in helping new leaders succeed. In "A Study of the Change Efforts Among First-Time High School Principals" (1989), Roberts and Wright provide an expanded view of the first-year priorities of beginning principals in the United States and Great Britain; their findings show that upon reaching their posts, these leaders focused first on student management, then on climate issues, and only later in the year on issues of vision, which they found most difficult to approach. Macmillan's "Approaches to Leadership Succession: What Comes with Experience?" (1993), which describes a study of five Canadian high school principals, concludes that older principals tend to avoid innovative ideas and leave novel approaches to their vice principals.

Three Experiences in Leadership Succession

To see how the process of leadership succession plays out at innovating schools, let's consider three different experiences.[1] The following cases are amalgams of actual examples from the field.

Example 1: Windot Elementary School

Windot was a successful school in a small metropolitan community where most teachers joined the principal in his pursuit of an integrated curriculum centered on the state's approach to comprehensive reform. Though there were some unhappy teachers on staff, parents appreciated the quality of teaching at the school and the central office provided its full support.

---

1   Because I've included both successes and controversies in the text, I have used pseudonyms as well as real names; either way, the cases discussed are all based on true experiences from real schools.

Because of his notable work and affiliation with a national curriculum project, Principal Robert Sandborn was given the chance to leave Windot and apply his ideas on a broader scale. Robert's departure presented Windot with the dilemma of having to replace a popular and accomplished leader. After a thorough selection process that included community input, the board eventually offered the principalship to Margery Calmento.

After coming to Windot, Margery studied the school's prior innovations and tried to understand the school's record in detail. She came to the conclusion that because the school was doing many things very well, a radical change of course was unnecessary. Still, there were many improvements that the staff could make to its current program that would move Windot to a higher level of performance. For instance, she decided to help teachers better understand their students' performance on standardized tests by helping them take apart test reports and link the results to their teaching practices. Because she went about this with the full support of teachers and in the spirit of continuing reform, her school's performance on assessments improved and Robert's work was carried forward. Margery clearly had an agenda of continuing previous reform.

Example 2: Bounty Elementary School

Under the leadership of Principal Andrea Sulaton, Bounty Elementary School became well known for its creative curriculum, and community service and student assessment programs. Because shared government was at the heart of the school's reform process, Andrea worked closely with faculty and staff to push Bounty to the next levels of development. Much to the delight of many community members, Bounty seemed set on a course of continuing progress even while other schools in the district were not. Success led to more success, and it was not long before Andrea found herself with an offer that was too good to pass up.

Just like Windot, Bounty was now forced to consider life without its beloved leader. Alice Bertrum, an honest, sincere, and dedicated educator, was eventually selected as the next principal. After carefully considering the situation at the school, she decided to support the shared governance structure, but gave some teachers the impression that she preferred a stronger hand. She also questioned some of the practices at the heart of Bounty's reform, at least according to faculty members who had initially supported her. Though Alice promoted what she considered to be bold new initiatives, it was not long before faculty and staff began to sense that the school was moving away from its reform program.

Example 3: Ruggers High School

Ruggers High School was deep into its reform program and had successfully adopted a national curriculum model when Principal Sarah Bellamy decided to retire after four mostly brilliant years of service. Sarah's long career could not have come to a more rewarding end, and she thought that this was exactly how one should leave the profession—on a high note. Following in her footsteps was Elliot Rodriguez, the seasoned vice principal of a neighboring school who had studied the Ruggers curriculum carefully and attended professional development training. When I spoke to Elliot, it was clear to me that he not only understood the concepts that undergirded the curriculum, but also deeply appreciated what the school's approach could do for its students. His intention was to carry forth Sarah's work carefully and methodically. If Sarah was the architect of Ruggers' program, Elliot was its gifted contractor and builder: under his leadership, the school's approach to curriculum was refined—curriculum and instruction planning was carried out to great effect and parents seemed to appreciate the school's efforts. I was therefore greatly surprised when I contacted the school two years later and found that some teachers felt things had become a bit stale. Though they admitted that the school was still on a positive course, the teachers said they no longer found Ruggers to be the exciting, pioneering place it had once been. Reform had become repetition in their eyes. Perhaps it was time for a new spark.

Action Strategy: An Evolutionary Leadership Choice Model

Combine the findings of research on transition, curriculum, and instruction and assessment activities and a picture of strategic choices in leadership emerges. (I have used the word "choice" because I believe that these are options that leaders may exercise as circumstances change. My hope is that leaders will use research such as the present work to decide to move in directions that are more likely to produce sustained growth for their organizations.) I will refer to this as the Evolutionary Leadership Choice Model (see Figure 1.1). As these schools progressed from the first year through to the end of the first decade of their course in restructuring, different leadership choices opened up, along with apparent consequences. These start with the first stage (Initiation or Tradition) where leaders and the group either embark on the course of transforming their school or elect a more traditional approach. By definition, innovating schools chose Initiation. This period typically lasts about five years. The second stage (Continuity or Mission Shift) begins with the departure of the founding leader and presents the choice of either building upon the restructuring directions of the founder or set-ting a different course. The third stage (Renewal or Perceived Stagnation) comes at the end of the first decade after restructuring has started, and involves a choice between continued incremental adjustments or break-ing through to a culture of faculty ownership of the vision, including taking major new steps towards its continued enhancement.

FIGURE 1.1
THE EVOLUTIONARY LEADERSHIP
CHOICE MODEL

Initiation		Tradition
Continuity	OR	Mission Shift
Renewal		Perceived Stagnation

Stage 1: Initiation or Tradition

Within five years or so, schools faced their first choice. Would they initiate restruc-turing or proceed with a business-as-usual approach? All schools in this book initiated profound changes. The profile of the leader was one of the visionary architect, although the specific vision changed with each setting. They were all high-energy individuals and demanded a great deal from themselves and their organizations. A common reaction to their time in office was excitement combined

in several cases with some weariness at the end of their tenure.

Stage 2: Continuity or Mission Shift

In the next phase, which lasts about two years, schools experienced two different kinds of leaders who sought to replace the founder. Bounty's experience was one of Mis-sion Shift. Their leader seems to have held a related but alternative vision to that of the founding leader. This was reflected in priori-ties and in leadership style. The reaction from the teachers dedicated to the restructuring started under the founder was one of opposi-tion. On the other hand, Windot experienced Continuity: The leader worked as a dedicated builder honoring the direction of the found-ing leader. The work was one of codifying and organizing rather than reinventing the mis-sion, and the result seems to be one of satis-faction on the part of the faculty and staff.

Stage 3: Renewal or Perceived Stagnation

In the third phase of development (start-ing around the ninth year), schools seemed to have new needs, thus raising new choices. Perceived Stagnation appears to be connected with leadership that follows the path of Con-tinuity from Stage 2; that is, the leader contin-ues to be the dedicated builder who concentrates on adjustments and mechanics. While this worked well in the earlier stage, continuing in this direction seems related to faculty members yearning for the glory days of the past and raising questions such as, "Are we drifting from the qualities that made us special?" This condition describes some trends at Ruggers.

The choice of Renewal comes when a faculty shows that it has internalized restructuring as a habit of being. Leadership in Renewal is still important, but leaders behave more like prime ministers open to power sharing. Goals include deep systemic work aimed at pushing the school to long-term, high-level results. There seemed to be a culture of teacher ownership of restructuring and renewed confidence in the teachers' ability to create a culture of reform that will outlast any given leader. There also appeared to be satisfaction with this stage of the journey.

Although the Evolutionary Leadership Choice Model, as applied to these cases, reflects experiences of multiple leaders at each school, this does not need to be the case. It may be possible for a single leader to transform from Continuity to Renewal. Further, the model is intended to help clarify leader behaviors and possible reactions to them inside of the school; it is not intended to account for all of the complexities schools face at the community, district, and state levels.

Making the Model Work for You

The Evolutionary Leadership Choice Model is designed to help you locate your school in the reform cycle and plan your next steps. Here's how to apply the model to your school.

First determine how long you have been involved in your current reform efforts. This might seem obvious if your program has been very formal, but many schools that have moved gradually toward reform might benefit from a dialogue about when the reforms began and where the school is in the process. Develop an expanding dialogue about the stage your school is at, the challenges and choices ahead of you, and what each choice means to your school. What do you, as a community, mean by initiation? Continuity? Renewal? How would you recognize these? Can you make them more easily observable? Are they measurable? Would your students, their families, and the wider community agree with your assessments?

For each year since reforms began, devote a large piece of paper to answering the following questions:

- What major reform was initiated?
- Who was involved?
- How did the reform evolve during the first year?
- Where was the reform successful?
- Where were the results less than satisfactory?
- What specific changes to student learning were recorded?

- What role did the school's leadership team play in the reform?

To ensure an accurate historical perspective, it would be best for a cross section of faculty, administration, and community to answer these questions together. After answering the questions above for each year, you may want to answer the following for the reform agenda in general:

- Where is there strong agreement or disagreement about the reform agenda at your school?
- How widespread has actual involvement in the reform agenda been?
- What different reasons are there for successes and failures regarding reforms? Can you identify a pattern?
- Have you maintained a record of student achievement as tied to specific reform efforts?
- How has leadership fit into your school's reform agenda?

Once you have devised a fairly coherent narrative of the reform agenda at your school thus far and analyzed your school's performance, it's time to see where you are on the continuum of stages in the Evolutionary Leadership Choice Model. For instance, if your group has seen a series of small, unrelated initiatives rather than a serious, sustained reform effort, then your school is at Stage 1 (Initiation or Tradition). In this case, you are likely to need a visionary architect if you decide to move ahead with reforms. Many of the ideas in the first two chapters of *Staying Centered* are designed to help you work through the early stages of reform; you may want to consult these along with other writings on school renewal if you are at Stage 1.

On the other hand, your analysis may show that your school's reforms are well under way. If you agree that change has been part of your plan for at least five years, and you are facing leadership succession, then your school is at Stage 2 (Continuity or Mission Shift) of the model. It is vital at this stage that you choose between continuity and mission shift. The schools I studied seemed to strongly favor maintaining their current direction with some fine-tuning of new programs.

The choices presented at Stage 2 bring to mind the writing of Thomas Kuhn (1962) on paradigms. If we consider the decision to move toward deep change as a kind of turning point, the shape of reform becomes a new model of schooling, or a new paradigm. Choosing continuity is a decision to live within the confines of that model and continue to refine it rather than to redefine it. The decision toward mission shift, however, is a strategic move in the opposite direction. It is possible that the whole reform direction has not had the intended results, or that circumstances beyond the school have created new imperatives. Mission shift after five or more years of reform is not necessarily an evil. But it is extremely important for there to be general agreement to change course. This is also a time to discuss the difference between *mission*—where we want the school to go based upon shared values and a shared vision—and *tactics*—strategies along the way to our shared vision. Changing tactics in light of new information may help to strengthen the current mission and may be the best possible move toward continuity.

Finally, your historical analysis of your school's reform agenda may show that there has been a decade-long process of successful reform that needs to be reconceived. One important reason that the schools in *Staying Centered* gave for starting their reform programs was the success that they had with the traditional model of schooling: morale was high, student achievement was equally impressive, the building was

in good shape, and the community was generally very supportive. Educators at these schools were like emerging athletes who can easily run five miles and are itching for the next challenge. Ironically, they felt that without a new challenge, performance would eventually deteriorate.

This is exactly how leaders at successfully reforming schools should feel after about a decade. Faculty members who have stretched to get their school this far may be hungry for something new to inspire them. Having realized its mission, the school's task is now to build an inspiring new vision.

Clearly, the Evolutionary Leadership Choice Model can help your school define the qualities required of your next leader. The visionary architect required at Stages 1 and 3 is quite different from the careful craftsperson necessary for working on reforms already in place at Stage 2.

2

Leadership Mentoring

Note: This chapter was adapted from the following source: Gross, S. J. (2002). Sustaining change through leadership mentoring at one reforming high school. *Journal of In-Service Education, 28*(1), 35–56. Reprinted by permission of Triangle Press.

Perspective

IN THE MID 1980S I BECAME A DIRECTOR OF CURRICULUM AND STAFF DEVELopment in a Vermont school district. One of my first duties was to help develop and coordinate a mentoring program for new faculty at our high school. Working with teachers, administrators, and board members, we created a project to help newly hired teachers by matching them with seasoned faculty members. Ours was an early example of a mentoring program; in the years since it was established, a growing realization that guidance into new and complex roles is essential has resulted in many programs that focus on mentoring new teachers.

Sadly, the same cannot be said about programs to help new principals. While some schools and districts have done fine work acquainting new leaders with the specific demands of their new role, they remain exceptions. The problem is compounded by the fact that leadership is often an isolating experience: Unlike their colleagues in the classroom, principals are normally without job-alike companions at work. Principals exist in other buildings in the district, of course, but their connections to each other may range from collegial to competitive, and they often have no vested interest in one another's success.

All of these difficulties are exacerbated, in my view, by the unique demands placed upon those attempting to replace the founding leaders in successfully reforming schools. Expectations are high, everyone is used to effective leadership, and the situation is almost by definition subject to rapid change and frequent bouts of turbulence. Therefore, any strategy that will help new leaders find their way and become grounded is important to consider.

Background

The idea of mentoring is ancient. The term itself dates back to Homer's *Odyssey*; as Boon (1998) reminds us, Mentor was entrusted with watching over King Odysseus's son, Telemachus, while Odysseus was at war. In modern times, businesses have used mentoring to help junior level employees advance.

The practice of mentoring is well known among aspiring principals. In "Benefits of a Mentoring Program for Aspiring Administrators" (1993), Daresh and Playko make the connection between educational and business mentoring. They also report that mentors tend to enjoy their roles as teachers of a new generation, and discuss the need to study how mentoring relationships are formed and maintained. Peel, Wallace, Buckner, Wrenn, and Evans highlight the need for the careful training of mentors in their article, "Improving

Leadership Preparation Programs Through a School, University, and Professional Organization Partnership" (1998). In *The Path to School Leadership: A Portable Mentor* (1993), Bolman and Deal use a case study of a new principal's first year and his reflections with a mentor to highlight five major lessons important to new principals: mapping a school's politics, empowering people, aligning the structure with the job at hand, celebrating the school's culture, and reframing a variety of perspectives to understand a problem.

Mentoring has also received international attention. Southworth discusses his study of mentors helping British school leaders in "Reflections on Mentoring for New School Leaders" (1995). He found that mentoring helps new leaders overcome isolation and allows the mentor and protégé to "consider and reconsider" events. Problems include finding a compatible pair and ensuring that mentoring prepares leaders for schools in the future, rather than socializing them to the practices of the past. In "Principalship Mentoring in Singapore: Who and What Benefits?" (1998) Boon discusses a study of mentoring in Singapore that found that mentors felt they had improved their professional knowledge by taking on their new roles, and that protégés became part of a wider network of colleagues while developing greater self-confidence. Coleman, Low, Bush, and Chew (1996) also studied mentoring, both in Great Britian and Singapore. They report that British school leaders appreciate working with nonjudgmental colleagues, and that there are important differences between the British and Singaporean systems, such as duration of the mentoring process. Erasmus and van der Westhuizen, who wrote guidelines for mentoring new principals in South Africa, advise that mentors' tasks should include consulting, guiding, and role modeling in their paper, "Guidelines for the Professional Development of School Principals by Means of a Mentoring System in a Developing Country" (1994).

A different group of studies examines mentoring from a gender perspective. In "Mentoring Partnerships: Key to Leadership Success for Principals and Managers" (1994), Matters describes a mentoring program in Australia designed to encourage more women to become school leaders. The author notes that the brevity of the program (it lasts two weeks) and a scarcity of female mentors are two problems that must be overcome. Pavan examined mentoring relationships in Pennsylvania schools and districts, and discusses her findings in "Mentors and Mentoring Functions Perceived as Helpful to Certified Aspiring and Incumbent Female and Male Public School Administrators" (1986). She too found that female mentors are scarce, and that teachers find psychosocial functions, such as support and encouragement, to be most helpful during mentoring. The Principal's Institute at Bank Street College (1992) focused on increasing the number of women

and minorities in leadership positions in public schools. Mentoring in this program lasted one semester and was considered to be the project's most useful aspect. Feedback from participants indicated that this preservice model would have been more useful if the mentoring relationship had been sustained for a longer period. In "Principal Mentoring Programs: Are School Districts Providing the Leadership?" (1992) Cohn and Sweeny discuss the role of school districts in establishing effective mentoring programs, especially for helping underrepresented groups such as women and minorities to become principals.

Other studies focus on mentoring for assistant principals who wish to become building leaders. In "The Principal as Mentor, Partner of Assistant Principals" (1989), Paskey discusses mentoring of assistant principals by their current principals and provides a general pattern for that relationship. Calabrese and Tucker-Ladd look at the kinds of issues that mentors should discuss with assistant principals in "The Principal and Assistant Principal: A Mentoring Relationship" (1991). They suggest that mentoring pairs take time each day to debrief and ask questions, and also discuss when and how mentoring relationships should end. In *Finding One's Way: How Mentoring Can Lead to Dynamic Partnership* (1998), Crow and Matthews describe peer mentoring for mid-career leaders and discuss a yearlong mentoring plan. In their opinion, patience, understanding, and tolerance are among the required qualities for mentors.

These studies help establish a strong background for mentoring new leaders. Yet the literature nearly always depicts cases of relatively short-lived mentor/protégé relationships in schools not engaging in innovation. By contrast, the example of Rosetta High School below focuses on a reforming school where an extended mentorship made a great deal of difference.

Leadership Mentoring at Rosetta High School

Rosetta High School is set high on a hill and overlooks much of the town of Eastford. Though Eastford is a growing community, Rosetta also draws from other communities in the district, such as Randolph, a much larger community with an urban orientation. At the time of my study, Rosetta had 760 students.

In the early 1990s the school completely changed its orientation, joining a national reform group and moving toward shared governance, greater input and responsibility for students in their own learning, and stronger connections with the community. The role of shared governance is of particular interest because many decisions at Rosetta were made by the Academic Council, a group comprised of faculty, administrators, parents, and

students and charged with key programmatic decision making.

Joan Singleton was the principal of Rosetta as it moved into its new identity. Her work included guiding the new school in the early years, establishing new norms and procedures, and representing the school in the community and among her peers and supervisors at the district level. Joan was highly successful as a principal, and Rosetta's first years as an innovative school went well.

Rosetta experienced leadership succession when Joan accepted an early retirement. Two years after her departure, Laura Johnston became principal. Both Laura and Joan were successful faculty members at Rosetta before becoming administrators, and shared backgrounds in counseling. As part of her early retirement agreement, Joan needed to perform some service for the district. After discussion with Laura and approval from the superintendent, Frank Moorely, the pair decided to enter into a sustained mentoring relationship.

The Five Stages of Mentoring

The duration of Joan and Laura's relationship was not established in advance, and was subject to review during an annual meeting between Laura, Joan, and Frank. In all, the district supported the mentoring relationship for three years.

Joan and Laura's relationship was different from most mentoring examples found in the literature. First, Joan and Laura were long-term colleagues and good friends. Second, their relationship was sustained longer than many of the previous cases, which usually lasted between a few weeks and a semester. And third, the intensity of the contact was greater. Joan and Laura spoke on the telephone nearly every night of the school year for about a half hour, and met for one afternoon each month. At the monthly meetings, they would fax a written agenda to Frank's office. Joan also helped facilitate faculty meetings periodically during the school year and in the summer.

It is important to note that Joan and Laura's relationship was purely voluntary on all sides. Laura had been a successful vice principal prior to becoming a principal. She was a trusted and valued member of the Rosetta community, and nearly everyone acknowledged her ability in her new role. Likewise, Joan had many other possible ways to serve the district during her early retirement years. Though she was lionized as a school leader, she was comfortable moving on after leaving Rosetta.

Because I conducted three of my interviews with Joan and Laura during their monthly meetings, I was able to listen in as they worked through typical issues together. In all three cases, I was able to ask questions about events at Rosetta and then listen for about 45 minutes as the pair carefully worked through one of the difficult issues then facing Laura. By transcribing the three sessions and carefully mapping the stages of dialogue between the pair, I found that Joan had carefully guided Laura through five stages of dialogue during each of the three meetings (see Figure 2.1).

Stage 1: Laying Out the Problem. In one session, Joan and Laura worked on a complex personnel problem dealing with grant funding of a part-time position for a faculty member. After Laura described the request, Joan started to help her see the complexity of the issue. Was this fair, or was this teacher trying to take advantage of the school's grant? First, she guided Laura through some of the chronology of the grant: How did the grant evolve? What was it intended to accomplish? Next, Joan helped Laura think the request through: What exactly does this person want? What is this person willing to do? What accountability would there be for this person? Finally, by fleshing-out the problem, Joan helped Laura uncover an ethical dilemma: If the request were granted, something else in the academic program might have to be cut. This, Laura believed, would not benefit students.

Stage 2: Gathering Crucial Data. After Laura's description of the issue, Joan pushed for more information. "One thing you have not talked about is hard data," she said. Joan helped Laura think about possible data sources. Whom could she trust to tell her accurate information? By this point

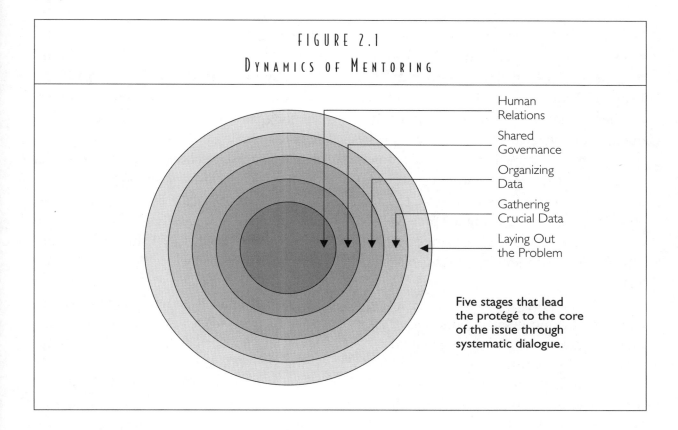

FIGURE 2.1
DYNAMICS OF MENTORING

Human Relations

Shared Governance

Organizing Data

Gathering Crucial Data

Laying Out the Problem

Five stages that lead the protégé to the core of the issue through systematic dialogue.

in the meeting, Laura and Joan had agreed on the dimensions of the problem, what facts were currently known, and what additional data was needed. Finally, Joan helped Laura devise a thoughtful and sensitive way of gathering more information before taking action, including a careful reading of the grant, examining minutes of academic council meetings, and holding informal individual meetings.

Stage 3: Organizing Data. Understanding the dimensions of a problem and working

from a well-rounded set of facts is an obvious and important step, but Joan did not stop there. By examining a constellation of additional issues relevant to the problem, she helped Laura to see a wider context and gain perspective. By understanding the size of the issue, Laura could more accurately communicate her needs to others.

Stage 4: Shared Governance. After helping Laura to understand and contextualize the issue, Joan helped her prepare to take it to the Academic Council. In this way, Joan kept faith with a key element of Rosetta's reform effort: the creation of site-based management and shared governance. Both Joan and Laura expressed great confidence in their school's model; Joan spoke frequently of the quality and fairness of the people on the council. She also acknowledged that the council should return to agreed-upon procedures from time to time. "If people are not following the process," she said, "Academic Council needs to revisit that. Site-based management does not mean anarchy."

Thinking through how to share a problem with the Academic Council so that it might be dealt with effectively required consideration. In the case of the personnel question described above, Joan suggested that the first step was to ask the council what information it needed to make a decision. Next, she suggested that Laura share the information that she had uncovered on the history of the issue. Third, Joan asked Laura to think of how the meeting might go. Because the teacher involved also sat on the council, was it fair for her to make her request and then participate in the discussion?

In the end, Joan and Laura concluded that the council needed to establish the process for making its decision. Laura was now ready to share the problem with the Academic Council, along with information and ideas that would help lead to a reasoned deliberation. Not only had the mentor and protégé thought through the issue at hand, they also showed faith in the school's reform structures in a way that they hoped might expand the Academic Council's effectiveness. Understanding how to share information with a decision-making board—whether it's an Academic Council, a school board, or a board of trustees—is a learned activity, and one that Joan understood well. By asking questions and pointing out possible roadblocks and opportunities, she helped Laura act both ethically and strategically.

Stage 5: Human Relations. In all three sessions I witnessed, Joan ended the discussion by raising human relations issues. She'd ask Laura to think about the worst that could happen—"What do you really have to fear?"—and to reflect upon her personal feelings about each of the parties involved. Having strong feelings was not a problem, but not acknowledging them could be a serious mistake. The personal side of the question was thus changed into a principle that could be dealt with by the Academic Council.

The five stages outlined above aimed to lift the level of Joan and Laura's discussion from ad hoc problem solving to careful examination of an issue, during which they could consider the possible consequences of different responses and transition the issue to the Academic Council. By repeating the stages, Joan seemed to have been sharing a habit of mind with Laura:

- Problems need to be examined in some detail,
- More information is often needed,
- Additional information needs to be organized carefully before acting,
- Assembled data has to be shared with someone or some group in an organized fashion, and
- The person or group has to be empowered to act in a responsible way.

My interviews with Joan and Laura revealed a reasoned, systematic approach to problem solving. The five stages flowed naturally from their meetings and resulted in a considered plan for action. The dialogues dealt with many aspects of the dilemmas, yet did not become stuck on any of them. The dedication of both mentor and protégé led to immediate results and long lasting improvements for Rosetta. Conversations with central office administrators showed that Laura had made rapid progress, and that the mentor-protégé program was really worth the investment of time and money. Clearly, using the five stages to organize mentoring is a strategy that innovating schools should consider.

Action Strategy: Mentoring Checklist

Clearly, the mentoring process at Rosetta had many impressive qualities. There was a carefully planned and sustained relationship between two professionals whose constant work helped keep the school's reforms on track despite the leadership succession. Here are some other characteristics that helped make the process work:

1. **Support from the top.** Rosetta's mentoring program was officially sanctioned by the school district and supervised by the superintendent. Each month an official agenda was submitted to the superintendent, who also conducted an annual review of the relationship in his office. This meant that the superintendent, mentor, and protégé needed to build time into their schedules to prepare for and conduct the annual review, as well as for developing standards for the continuation of the mentoring process.

2. **Room in the budget.** This mentoring model cost about $2,500 per year and was paid for out of the district's operating budget.

3. **A formal role for the mentor.** The mentor in this case was acting in an official capacity in line with her early retirement responsibilities. A commitment of time on her part was expected and understood.

4. **A formalized process.** This model called for very frequent contact between the mentor and the protégé. In addition to daily phone conversations, the pair met face-to-face once a

month for about four hours. This meant Joan and Laura had to commit to about 16 hours of contact time (not including time to prepare for and debrief after meetings). The fact that they were friends did not diminish the need for formal procedures, but rather underscored the fact that attending to the business of school leadership remained paramount.

5. **A strong commitment to the school's reform process.** Student learning was the top priority throughout the mentoring relationship, and structures central to Rosetta's reform program helped keep the mentoring focused.

6. **A strong commitment to the new principal's professional development.** Matching the emphasis on school reform was an equal concern for Laura's professional development and well-being.

7. **A commitment of adequate time.** The mentoring program at Rosetta was highly unusual because it took three years to complete. By allowing the mentoring to continue through several academic years, problems that were part of the normal school cycle (e.g., student count in September) could be distinguished from one-time events. Just as important, the lengthy duration allowed the mentor and protégé the luxury of seeing the larger picture—a perspective that helped them both better understand the school, its reform process, their own evolving professional lives, and the effect of the wider world on the issues at hand.

8. **Mentoring during an appropriate stage of the school's reform cycle.** It is clear that Rosetta High School was at Stage 2 (Continuity or Mission Shift) of the Evolutionary Leadership Choice Model. By having the outgoing principal mentor her replacement, the school chose to emphasize continuity over mission shift. This choice was indispensable for choosing the right mentor and protégé. Joan was a highly effective mentor in this case partly because she was the founding leader of the school's reform program. If the school community had chosen mission shift, the choice of the founding leader might not have been so obvious. Thus it is wise for administrators to consider the broad picture when selecting effective mentors.

Review the eight characteristics above. Forming a checklist of your own, sort them into the following categories:

- **Items that are already part of your school's operation.** Perhaps you do not have the exact same characteristics, but you have quite similar ones. This category will help you see two things: that you are probably on your way to having a leadership mentoring program in your district, even if you have only one of the elements in place now; and how to determine and prioritize the next steps in the formation of a mentoring program.

- **Items that you could easily put into place in the next academic year.** These are ideas that already have, or could easily gain, administrative- or board-level support. For each item in this category, discuss and diagram the steps necessary for implementing it, including crucial conversations, support-building strategies, financial considerations, and especially professional development.

- **Items that will not come to you easily.** First, map out what you will have in place after dealing with the items in the previous two categories. This will show you the whole as well as the missing pieces of your program, and will make it easier for you to judge whether or not your program will be viable. Next, you will need to adapt the items to your circumstances. For example, you may be able to create a support system for the new principal that lasts one year but not three. You will need to judge if this is a critical flaw or not. It may be wise to proceed with the one-year program, carefully document it, and judge whether it should continue as the process unfolds. Perhaps you do not have the services of a successful retiring leader. In this case, your mentoring program should be modified to recruit leader mentors.

Once you have worked through the steps of this exercise, you will be able to more easily see what steps your own setting requires before making leadership mentoring part of your district's practice. Use the Leadership Mentoring Readiness Table (Figure 2.2) to see what actions you may need to take soon.

FIGURE 2.2
LEADERSHIP MENTORING READINESS TABLE

Checklist Item	Items in Place	Items Easily Put in Place	Items That Will Take Time to Put in Place
1. Support from the top			
2. Room in the budget			
3. A formal role for the mentor			
4. A formalized process			
5. A strong commitment to the school's reform process			
6. A strong commitment to the new principal's professional development			
7. A commitment of adequate time			
8. Mentoring during an appropriate stage of the school's reform cycle			

Teachers as School Leaders

3

Perspective

DURING THE LATE 1980S, OTTER VALLEY UNION HIGH SCHOOL WAS ONE OF only a few in Vermont to undergo a serious restructuring effort. Like others of that era, Otter Valley's reforms included interdisciplinary instruction, portfolio assessment, a switch from tracking to heterogeneous grouping, and the collection of baseline academic information to be shared with the community. The restructuring effort also placed the school in a partnership with the University of Vermont, which used Otter Valley Union as a site for graduate coursework.

In late spring of 1990, while Otter Valley Union was in the midst of rapid change, both the principal and assistant principal sought and found promotions in other schools. Although their departures did not reflect a disagreement with the direction of the school, it did represent a serious challenge. Who would lead the school at such a creative yet turbulent time? The eventual answer was three teachers with a shared principalship.

This chapter tells the story of the three principals' rise to authority and their work, especially in restructuring, during their first year. Specifically, I will address three sets of questions:

1. How did the leaders deal with the issue of leadership for innovation?
2. In what way did they act as team builders?

3. To what extent was this teacher leadership example similar to earlier models?

Background

There is a historical context for the Otter Valley Union experience in the literature on teacher power. According to Beck and Murphy (1995), in 1916 there were 200,000 public schools in the United States, each with a single teacher for all grades. The one-room schoolhouse represented a kind of teacher power, in that teachers were in control of their building. Although clear limits to this power existed in the form of outside supervision, community pressure, and even the normally low standing and poor salary of teachers at the time, these teachers did exercise considerable control within their realm. Anarchist-inspired experimental schools, such as those connected to the Modern School movement of the early 20th century, also had teacher-leaders; at New York's Ferrer School, the young Will Durant—later a renowned writer of popular history books—carried the title of Principal and Teacher.

During the same period, John Dewey called for giving teachers more power to actually run their schools, linking teacher decision-making power to the cause of democracy itself:

Until the public school system is organized in such a way that every teacher has some regular and representative way in which he or she can register judgment upon matters of educational importance, with the assurance that this judgment will somehow affect the school system, the assertion that the present is not, from the internal standpoint, democratic seems to be justified. (1903, p. 126)

Dewey's colleague in Chicago, Ella Flagg Young—the nation's first female superintendent of a large city school system—promoted a particular form of teacher power by inventing teacher councils in the early 20th century. These were meant to include all teachers and the principal, and the original councils in Chicago were charged with looking into curricular as well as general education questions. Like Dewey, Young also drew an analogy with democracy, noting that "a Democracy whose school system lacks confidence in the ability of the teachers to be active participants in planning its aims and methods is a logical contradiction of itself" (Webb & McCarthy, 1998, p. 227).

Although the first councils held promise, they represented only part of the political and economic dynamic alive in the society. There were powerful conflicting forces at work: Local democracy and teacher councils were directly at odds with the efficiency model of centralized authority and scientific management, and as Beck and Murphy note, "Democracy versus efficiency would become one of the key sets of powerful oppositional forces in schooling throughout the 20th century" (p. 99). Ella Flagg Young showed an awareness of this issue when she spoke about the contradiction of calling for public schools to promote democracy on the one hand, while having them run by elites of society on the other: "Why talk about the public school as an indispensable requisite of a Democracy and then conduct it as a prop for an Aristocracy?" (Webb & McCarthy, p. 228).

The democratic administration movement of the 1930s and 1940s provided another call for teachers to assume greater power. Koopman, Miel, and Misner's *Democracy in School Administration* (1943), for example, had a clear antitotalitarian, prodemocracy bent, perfectly suited for the wartime United States. The sentiment behind the book was that democratic institutions could produce like-minded young citizens. The foreword, by S. A. Courtis, speaks of the clear attempt to save democracy from "chaos, fascism, communism and dictatorship" (p. ix), and the editor's note calls for democratizing administration as "a natural outgrowth of earlier democratic development in the American public schools" (p. xiii). Though the book does not push for replacing administrators with teachers, it calls for administrators, teachers, students, and community adults to "participate democratically" not only in areas

of instruction but in budget, personnel, "and other so-called administrative problems, all of which have their bearing in instruction" (p. 11). According to the authors, administrators should not "abdicate their positions" (p. 9), but rather foster leadership in others, namely teachers, students, and community adults.

Recent Research

In their article "In Ontario: Preparing Teachers to Be Leaders," Anderson, Rolheiser, and Gordon (1998) respond to the question of teacher preparation for leadership roles by documenting a Canadian teacher education program that emphasizes school improvement skills. The article raises the issue of how to define the task of teaching, and challenges the tradition of separating the role of teaching from that of leading school-wide reform. Packard and Bas-Isaac describe a sequential teacher development and leadership model that advocates mentoring, peer coaching, and clinical development in "Educational Change and Reform: An Integrated Model for the Professional Development of Teacher Leaders" (1988).

In "Who Will Lead? The Top Ten Factors that Influence Teachers Moving into Administration" (1999), Cooley and Shen present the results of a survey of 189 midwestern graduate students enrolled in educational administration courses. Factors attracting these students to schools included the reputation of the superintendent (sixth most important), the level of community support (the third most important), and the relationship among the board, administration, and teachers (single most important).

Do teacher-leaders behave any differently from traditional administrators? Adam Urbanski's leadership of teacher union efforts in Rochester, New York, during the 1990s is well known for its emphasis on reform and innovation. In "Reflections on Teachers as Leaders" (1997), Urbanski and Nickolaou speak of teacher leadership as collegial, with a focus on learning and a larger purpose of freeing teachers as a group, rather than managing them. Lambert, Collay, Dietz, and Kent discuss the need for teacher-leaders to emphasize constructivist approaches in their book, *Who Will Save Our Schools? Teachers as Constructivist Leaders* (1997). The authors imply that schools should promote learning opportunities for everyone in the organization, in addition to significant staff development. In "Teachers as Leaders: Hope for the Future" (1994), Mooney advocates teacher leadership as a way out of isolation and into a community. He asserts that teacher-leaders are more likely than administrators to be sensitive to the needs of faculty, to understand the realities of the classroom, and to lead as coaches rather than in a more hierarchical fashion.

Lieberman, Falk, and Alexander studied six New York City elementary schools where teacher-leaders replaced traditional principals and published their results in *A Culture in the Making: Leadership in Learner-Centered Schools* (1994). The leaders they studied were focused on administrative skills (keeping track of buses, paperwork, and academic schedules), political skills (educating and negotiating with stakeholders), and pedagogical understandings (providing ongoing professional development). In *Teachers as Leaders: Is the Principal Really Needed?* (1997), Creighton examines an elementary school in Casper, Wyoming, where the principal was replaced by pairs of teachers who worked on typical administration issues such as budget, board and community relations, and curriculum.

In my own case study on leadership succession, "Life After Moses: The Fate of Selected Innovative Institutions Beyond the Transformational Leader" (1999), I discussed another school where a pair of teachers served as principals. Each teacher-principal was given responsibility for half of the rural K–12 school and retained about half of her teaching responsibilities. The curriculum, instructional, and assessment reforms that this school had been very actively involved with continued during this time, but the teacher-principal system was eventually deemed unworkable and was changed back to a traditional principal model. Even with two teacher-principals, the demands of administration and significant classroom responsibilities were too much. Both teacher-principals felt drained of energy.

Teachers as Leaders at Otter Valley Union High School

Otter Valley Union High School is located in Brandon, Vermont, a community of about 4,000 residents. At the time of my study, there were about 700 students at the school in grades 7–12, from five elementary schools in small towns and farming communities.

According to an article in the school newsletter called "The History of Restructuring," (1990) Superintendent William Mathis initiated restructuring efforts in the district in the spring of 1989 by encouraging the faculty to rethink its approach to education. That same spring, 15 faculty members and two community members served on a committee charged with economic and business outreach.

The school applied for and received a $10,000 grant from the state to support restructuring efforts. School and community members attended statewide meetings and considered different approaches, such as the Copernican plan and detracking efforts demonstrated by a high school in Massachusetts. A professor from the University of Vermont was brought to the final faculty meeting to help organize reform strategies, where the teachers agreed to work on interdisciplinary studies, scheduling, and community relations.

Against this backdrop of sustained and reasonably intense reform, the departure of the school's principal and assistant principal was announced. Although people were happy that these two talented administrators had found exciting new positions, the problem of leadership at Otter Valley Union loomed large. In a creative response, school and district leaders looked to the faculty for leadership. One teacher was selected because of past administrative experience; another held an administrative certificate and experience as a guidance counselor; and the third, an English teacher, was well known for her organizational skills. Because there were now three leaders, the team became known as "the troika."

The troika leaders shared two reasons for becoming teacher-principals. First, they all had a long-term relationship with the school; one had been a student there, and another had spent his entire career at the school. Both had seen leaders come and go, but wanted to put some of their own ideas into action. The third member of the troika said that while she thought she would never leave the English classroom, she was willing to do so in order to work with the other two leaders.

Being senior faculty members seems to have played a part in the teachers' decision to move into leadership positions. They calculated that between them they had over 75 years of experience; one spoke about being glad to have this challenge after years in the classroom and in smaller administrative roles. The troika opportunity fit an empty space and clearly meant that things were not going to become boring. When I interviewed the leaders, all three shared a common sense of the school and its community. Otter Valley Union was not an easy place in their eyes; many students were poor or from difficult homes. Yet the leaders were proud of the school, the community, and their fellow teachers.

The restructuring process at Otter Valley Union continued under the troika. At the time of the leaders' ascension to their posts, the reform agenda was clearly focused on student learning and included such goals as higher achievement, pursuit of a vocation, global awareness, and helping learners see the interconnectedness of subject matter. These goals were organized into four large categories: Higher Academic Achievement, Improved Student Attitudes, Increased Community Involvement, and Equity. Data were assembled in each category to become part of an action research cycle.

With the help of a university course in school development, all teachers and administrators joined teams known as "families of learners" (see Figure 3.1). This structure was linked to the restructuring goal of creating schools-within-a-school and was intended to foster a sense of community. Representatives of each team met with the troika leaders once a week. The faculty also agreed to work in

nine different committees, each focused on a different dimension of the school reform agenda, including action research, scheduling, and in-service training. New restructuring plans were designed to bring teachers, administrators, students, and board members together in new ways, all under the guidance of the three teacher leaders.

The school soon settled into a pattern of pursuing the school's reform goals. The Action Research Committee's report after the first year of troika leadership included the number of honor roll students and detentions for the year, as well as standardized test and SAT scores for 10th, 11th, and 12th grade students. The report also contained results from surveys of students, teachers, parents, and community members, who appeared satisfied with the troika and the school's academic program. Both parents and students gave the school's leadership team high marks for approachability and for allowing parent input into administrative decisions. Teachers were also highly supportive, and said they appreciated the degree to which the troika leaders were visible and available. There were also reports of improved morale and student discipline. Feedback from all surveys was analyzed carefully and became the basis for planning future directions for the team.

Although the troika arrangement was unusual, the leaders at Otter Valley Union did share the following important traits with other leaders at innovative schools:

- The choice of three veteran educators new to administration matches up with the research on innovation and succession (see Creighton, 1997; Koopman, Miel, & Misner, 1943; and Lieberman, Falk, & Alexander, 1994).

- Once in place, the troika emphasized patterns of behavior that are strongly recommended by researchers, including vision, commitment, and teaming.
- The restructuring effort itself was meant to drastically change the

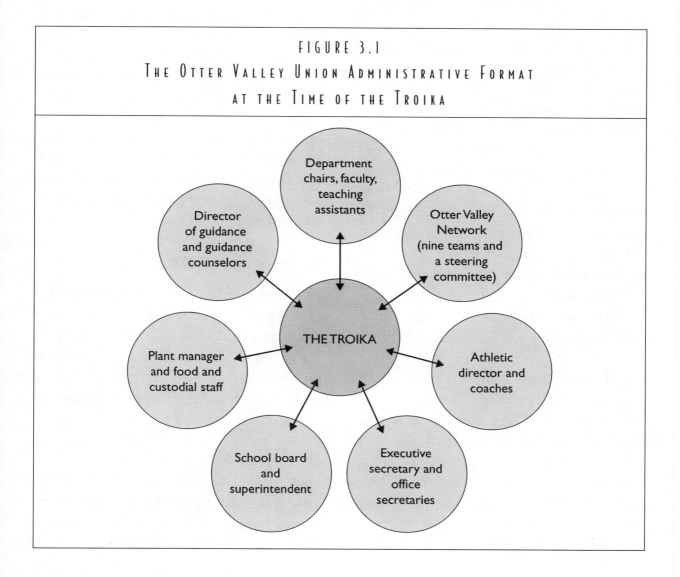

FIGURE 3.1
THE OTTER VALLEY UNION ADMINISTRATIVE FORMAT
AT THE TIME OF THE TROIKA

school's direction—the sheer depth of participation makes the troika an example of transformational leadership.

- The troika clearly led a site-based management institution.

The troika was organized as an effective team and worked with other highly organized staff members to pursue restructuring goals. This kind of organization does not appear to reflect industry trends at the time, but rather a shared concern for role clarification and alignment among all staff. Troika members and teachers, nearly all of whom participated on a restructuring team, had clearly defined roles and duties. In another departure from industry parallels, there was no sense from the data that teachers resented three of their own moving to positions of leadership; indeed, the opposite seems to have been the case.

Reflecting back on the Evolutionary Leadership Choice Model, the Otter Valley Union troika is an example of continuity rather than mission shift. These leaders helped their school move ahead with its reforms—their activities helped the change process already underway become deeper and more widely practiced. At a time of great need, the Otter Valley Union troika served as a crucial leadership bridge and stayed in operation long enough to make its mark on the school's administrative style, even after a more traditional principal was hired years later.

Action Strategy: Leadership Internship Program

As we have seen, teacher teams can provide crucial leadership during pivotal moments in the life of an innovating school. Though our examples focus on this strategy as a bridge between more traditional forms of leadership, this does not necessarily have to be the case. Regardless of the duration of teacher leadership, it is important to identify possible teacher-leaders and for them to become familiar with the leadership activities of their school. Shared governance, discussed in detail in Challenge 3, certainly helps in this orientation process. The purpose of this "Action Strategy" exercise is to help faculty members see the school from the principal's perspective by serving as interns for an administrator.

The Divisions of Internship

Compared to some other professional development activities, interning requires an extended allotment of time. Merely shadowing an administrator will not likely help an inexperienced person understand how to skillfully study and resolve problems, nor will a long but ill-designed program really give a novice leader a well-rounded grasp of the issues she will be facing. The work of an intern should, therefore, be divided into six areas with about equal time devoted to each. The suggested six elements of the leadership internship program are as follows:

1. **Curriculum, Instruction, and Assessment.** These are at the heart of the learning program at any school.

2. **Personnel.** The individuals who share the learning program with students in a proactive, collegial fashion.

3. **Community Relations.** The connection between the school program and parents and the wider community through dialogue and active engagement in further reform efforts.

4. **Resource Management.** This includes not only traditional budget operations, but also foundation and government support for innovative programs.

5. **External Affairs.** The school's relationship with outside organizations such as the district, state government, and board of directors.

6. **Physical Structure.** This is traditionally referred to as the school plant. Naturally it is vital for leaders to understand how the heating system operates, at least in principle, and to be aware of any safety issues. They should also understand the connection between a building's design and its educational mission. The intern needs to have a solid grasp of architecture and of the latest concepts in space planning to benefit the learning process.

The internship needs to include all of these items, discussed at a level slightly higher than the intern's previous experiences. Internship tasks should match the intern's skill level, and should further the authentic needs of the reforming school at the time of the internship.

The internship should last about one semester and should include about 100 hours of intern work, with weekly meetings between the intern and the mentor. Because this is a serious program that requires a good deal of time and effort, it deserves some kind of compensation, whether from the board or from a grant. The internship might also be part of a professional growth experience plan required by the state or district. If organized with a university or college program, the internship might even count as course credit for the intern—though both the intern and the mentor deserve professional recognition for their efforts.

Applying the Program

The goal of the internship program is to foster leadership skills among faculty in an innovating school. This may lead to a small group of faculty actually assuming the role of principal, as we saw in the case of Otter Valley Union, but it may also mean that the administrative skills of a large group of teachers are enhanced, thereby furthering reform. After selecting teachers and administrators to take part in the internship, school officials should take the following steps to bring the program to life:

1. After looking over the six elements of the leadership internship experience, the intern lists relevant previous experiences in a readiness sheet (see Figure 3.2). This accomplishes two things: It helps the mentor understand the relative strengths that the intern brings to the task, and it ensures that the internship is based upon new learning rather than on repeating earlier work.

2. The intern and mentor (likely to be the principal or assistant principal) discuss general projects to work on in the six key areas. It is important that this step not be one of dumping work onto a novice, but rather one in which a leader-in-training takes on new tasks as part of a leadership team. Planning

FIGURE 3.2
LEADERSHIP INTERNSHIP READINESS SHEET

The Six Elements	Previous Experience	New Experiences
Curriculum-Instruction-Assessment		
Personnel		
Community Relations		
Resource Management		
External Affairs		
Physical Structure		

for these tasks should include specific expectations, time requirements, necessary resources, and names of other staff members involved.

3. The intern keeps a journal, making entries at least twice a week. The experiences of leadership will probably vary. Sometimes it will be surprisingly inspiring; other times, even minimal progress will seem elusive. Journal passages will help the intern see her course through the early times just as she experienced them; the journal itself will also act as a core element of the internship portfolio (see Step 6).

4. The intern signs off on a weekly timesheet that contains a brief description of activities and accomplishments in the six key areas. The point of the timesheet is to show how this valuable semester was spent, and to offer those funding the internship program (e.g., the school board) a measure of accountability.

5. Because the internship program will probably succeed or fail depending on the quality of the relationship between the intern and the mentor, the two need to be in continuous contact. This includes daily conversations, of course, but also structured weekly meetings wherein intern and mentor review each project area, take notes, and conduct problem-solving exercises. Because it is all too easy for other pressing tasks to overwhelm the mentor, these meetings should be formalized, and should culminate in an end-of-semester review.

6. The intern builds a portfolio of experience, with the chief goal of demonstrating growth over time in each of the six areas. Evidence of this may include self-reflections, letters of recommendation, photographs of projects, descriptions of programs developed as part of the internship, timesheets, and journal entries.

Conclusion to Challenge 1

As we have seen, leadership succession is not a matter of *if* but of *when*. No matter how well our current leaders do their work, their departures are inevitable, and will perhaps occur sooner than anyone suspects. Accepting this fact means accepting a degree of turbulence, since losing a well-respected leader is painful for nearly everyone. Some turbulence can be useful, as it can energize an organization and provide the spark needed to mount a serious search for someone new. Understanding the patterns of leadership succession at reforming schools can directly affect how much turbulence a reforming school experiences.

I hope that the Evolutionary Leadership Choice Model in Chapter 1 has helped you to see the big picture for your school. Once the new leader is in place, there is a great deal for everyone to learn. Supporting a new principal through mentoring can make a crucial difference, as shown in Chapter 2, and it is neither costly nor esoteric. If school officials can't find an adequate replacement for the outgoing principal, they should seriously consider teacher leadership as a strategic bridge (see Chapter 3) rather than make a questionable decision just to have the office filled.

By using these three strategies, your innovative school may be able to face the fact of leadership succession in a planned and constructive fashion, and avoid serious mistakes that could cost the school and community irreplaceable time and energy. Individuals in leadership positions may have to change, but that does not mean that the act of leading needs to be placed at risk.

Challenge 2

What we obtain too cheaply, we esteem too lightly: 'tis dearness only that gives everything its value. Heaven knows how to place a proper price on its goods; and it would be strange indeed if so celestial an article as FREEDOM should not be highly rated.

—*Thomas Paine*

Keeping the Learning Agenda Alive

FIGURE C-2
TURBULENCE GAUGE FOR CHALLENGE 2

Degree of Turbulence	General Definition	Relevant Scenario
Light	Associated with ongoing issues Little or no disruption to the normal work environment Subtle signs of stress	Time goes on, but no new expectations for enhanced academic performance are placed on the school, which remains the same size as when the reforms were initiated. A consensus exists on most key questions.
Moderate	Widespread awareness of the issue and its specific origins	New academic performance goals are set that are in harmony with the mission, which most still agree with. The school is growing, reflecting a need to equal others in the district. There is no serious dislocation in the near future, and most teachers are still very involved in reform.
Severe	Possibility of large-scale community demonstrations A sense of crisis	New goals do not match the old mission very well, yet are rising faster than most feel is reasonable. The school's growth is getting out of control. Many staff members are leaving, and participation in shared governance seems to be losing support.
Extreme	Structural damage to the school's reform Collapse of the reform seems likely	Expectations for success far outstrip any reasonable possibilities. The student population has risen so dramatically that the nature of the school has changed and become very unfamiliar to the staff. There is no consensus among teachers and administrators as factions seem to overwhelm the agenda.

Challenge 2

Avoiding rapid growth and understanding rising expectations are both keys to staying focused on a mission. The two issues are like Scylla and Charybdis, the dangerous obstacles facing Odysseus on his travels back to Ithaca from the Trojan wars: On one side is the monster, on the other the whirlpool; either one may be enough of a strain to slow and even destroy reform. The leadership team—by which I mean everyone in the school and community who is either directly or indirectly involved in succession—should not navigate fearfully and defensively to avoid these dangers. The strategies in this section are designed to help you and your colleagues understand the forces behind dangerous growth and unrealistic expectations in a way that will help you to act in time.

A third issue that we will explore in this section is that of staying focused on your vision for the future. Reforming a school is not just a goal or a process. Research shows that continuous reform that responds successfully to rapidly changing conditions is more like a way of life than anything else (Gross, 1998). Just as living in a democracy means more than establishing a representative government and creating a constitution, working in a reforming school means being in a state of continuous development. As with all successful democracies, reforming schools need to have real platforms from which stakeholders can build, share, and work through long- and short-term agendas. In this section, we will look closely at the continuing efforts of shared governance models in two schools with long records of sustained innovation.

Before reading any further, look at the Turbulence Gauge in Figure C-2 and compare it to your own setting.

4 Dealing with Rapid Growth

THE CONCEPT OF GROWTH IS MARBLED INTO MANY ASPECTS OF LIFE IN THE United States. In the business world, for example, a growing share of the market usually leads to a rise in company profits. In other words, we tend to consider success and growth to be synonymous. After all, what positive venture can you think of that shows its results by shrinking?

Yet there are clear limits to this orientation. One day while walking near the picturesque Robert Frost trail in Ripton, Vermont, I listened to a biologist friend criticize the mentality of constant growth.

"Steve, the only thing that continues to grow without controls in nature is cancer," he said. "And cancer, unchecked, eventually kills its host."

Looked at another way, though businesses often claim that they want to maximize growth, they need to understand the serious risks that rapid growth almost always entails. However, the implication is clear: growth is fine, up to a point. Balance and harmony must lie at the heart of our expectations for our schools, and we need to help members of the school community who are not educators to understand that there are limits to business comparisons. We are working with children.

Naturally, some growth is not only understandable but a desirable part of the system and the plans of reforming schools. The early years of reform described in *Staying Centered* depict this situation clearly. Schools like Oceana High School in the San Francisco Bay area were asked to reinvent themselves starting on a very small scale. There was general agreement that the shrinking of the school to a very manageable size was

38

necessary. Fewer teachers would mean a coherent vision shared by a spirited team who wanted to engage in the hard work of inventing and experimenting.

In a way, the small size of many reforming schools in the early stages serves to protect and nurture fledgling laboratories of innovation. One familiar example of this behavior in the business world is the rise of the Macintosh computer, which began as a protected experiment at the Apple Computer company. But much as the Mac was expected to pull its own weight upon maturity, reforming schools are not exempt from careful scrutiny for very long. Typically, schools are expected to grow to the average size for the district within a few years, usually in incremental steps—an expectation that the schools I studied factored into their reform plans from nearly the beginning. Such growth raises the following crucial questions that need to be worked through very carefully if the integrity of the original reform is to be sustained:

What is motivating the desire to grow the reforming school in the first place? Are resources equitably distributed among all children in the district? Is the purpose control through economies of scale in the reforming school? Is there a desire to share the benefits presumed to exist in the innovating school with more students?

What is the timeline for growth? Who created the timeline? Is it reasonable?

What is meant by growth? For instance, is it reasonable to expect all schools at the same level to have roughly the same number of students? If the physical plants and curriculum-instruction-assessment patterns are equivalent, this might be a reasonable conclusion. However, the purpose of initiating reform efforts in the first place is often to disrupt the generic quality of the existing learning program. Would growth then necessarily result in sameness of size?

The two guiding words in this chapter are rapid and growth. Rapid can be a highly relative term: What is overly rapid to the busy building administrator may be minimally responsive to a board member or central office budget manager calculating per-pupil costs in the district. Adding 200 students to a school in its second year of reform may be extremely challenging to the principal whose primary focus is individualized instruction. To those looking at costs of student-teacher ratios at the central office and board level, such a change may be the smallest acceptable change in what they consider to be the right direction. Although the intention from all sides was usually sincere, the reforming schools in *Staying Centered* that were allowed to start off as small experiments did not generally have the benefit of carefully designed growth studies that included rationales for increases in students, faculty, and staff over time.

Figure 4.1 will help you place your own school into perspective.

FIGURE 4.1
GROWTH PRESSURES AT YOUR SCHOOL

Take a few minutes to note where the growth plan for your school
falls on the following scales:

1. The underlying motivation for growth is:

Ethical/Sharing   Purely Financial

    1   2   3   4   5

2. The timeline for growth:

Is reasonable and agreed to by local and   Results from an imposed
district educators as well as the public   plan with little local support

    1   2   3   4   5

3. The growth plan:

Takes the specifics of our schools'   Is generic, showing little
Curriculum-Instruction-Assessment   or no concern for the needs
work into consideration   or concerns of individual schools

    1   2   3   4   5

Perspective

Although I normally do not dwell on stories about disrupted reform, I believe that there is a need here to describe the case of a school we will call Bodsworth, as it very clearly embodies the serious challenge of overly rapid growth upon schools that were top performers. Lessons from this push for growth are legion, for both the building leadership and the district office.

Bodworth is an elementary school in an inner city serving black and Latino students. With the encouragement of the district superintendent and a nationally recognized reform curriculum, the school opened with an air of enthusiasm and confidence. Starting off small was an agreed-upon strategy for the school, so when I first visited there were fewer than 500 students in grades K–5. Student-teacher ratios were still challenging, with many classes having nearly 30 students. Still, things seemed to be working. The structure of the curriculum, strong professional development, a sophisticated technology backbone, and wonderful school-parent relations, were all easy to see. Equally impressive was the great team spirit. Teachers worked together to write units that integrated standards with engaging hands-on learning. Faculty knew about the successful work of colleagues and found ways to support one another's work. Progress moving students towards agreed-upon learning goals seemed evident to teachers, parents, and most important of all, students. Even the grounds seemed to be transformed, with members of the community coming on weekends to clean up litter and replace ignored weed beds with gardens. From the district level on down, Bodsworth was a source of pride.

It was two years until I was able to visit again. When I did, I might as well have been at a completely different institution. Gone were the old curriculum and sense of pride in the work of the faculty. In their place was a disheartened staff of veterans and a group of new teachers who did not relate to the program and practices that had once been so promising. Many reasons surfaced for the extreme turbulence that Bodsworth faced, including the loss of support from the central office with the departure of the district superintendent. However, the one factor that stood out as pivotal was the issue of growth. Because of its initial success, the school was scheduled to grow—indeed, pressure from parents who wanted their children to attend Bodsworth made growth inevitable. Soon things started to get out of hand. The K–5

pattern was changed to K–6, then K–8. Though school leaders and faculty tried to resist this decision, it was all but useless. New faculty and many new parents had to be brought into the Bodsworth family all at once.

Growth also meant that Bodsworth changed from being a public school of choice to an assigned school. Students from families that did not understand or agree with the school's curriculum started to enroll. If this growth had been gradual, things might have been different. However, when I spoke with faculty and watched students in class, I felt that I was witnessing an innovation being swamped faster than anyone could possibly bail. Bodsworth may have been doing many noble things for children even then, but the high-quality curriculum-instruction-assessment that I had once admired was all but impossible to see. Very rapid growth seemed a mortal blow to this experiment.

Action Strategy: Negative and Positive Feedback Loops

The story of Bodsworth Elementary shows the results of imposed rapid growth. As you can see, the pressures posed by the demand for more students, staff, teachers, and grade levels were stressful to those who originated the plan and had severe consequences for the entire reform effort. During my site visit, the principal told me that she regretted not fighting back with greater strength when the plans for growth were first proposed. I sympathized with this skilled and thoughtful leader, but wondered what tools she could have used to be more persuasive, especially in a large district such as hers.

The first task for leaders in reforming schools and districts should be to gain a larger picture of the forces pushing for growth. Sincere leaders at all levels want to do the right thing for students, but may come to very different conclusions when the time comes to design growth plans for the innovative school in their midst. In these cases, understanding the role of positive and negative feedback loops (Morgan, 1997; Senge, 1990) is vital in seeing the big picture (see Figures 4.2 and 4.3).

A Cause for Concern: The Positive Feedback Loop

Spinning out of control is a phrase that is both familiar and likely to create nervousness. Like a car flying wildly on ice, things that are out of control are dangerous and can often lead to wreckage. These are cases of severe or extreme turbulence, placing an entire operation at risk. The concept of the positive feedback loop helps to describe the underlying conditions of such situations.

One example of extreme turbulence due to rapid growth occurs when a foreign weed is introduced into an environment free of the weed's natural enemies. Here in Vermont, the weed is an aggressive vine introduced into New England. The vine pops up near a tree and takes it over, eventually killing it. Then it sinks its roots into surrounding areas, growing by neighboring trees that will share the same fate as the first one. The stronger the weed becomes, the more prolific the number of roots and vines invading native trees, and the greater the threat to many aspects of the habitat. The growth of the weed is not linear; it becomes a much greater problem and feeds upon itself as it develops. The more it grows, the greater the magnitude of the infestation.

Runaway inflation is another example of the problem. When prices are high, people ask for higher wages to keep up with the cost of goods and services, which cause higher costs for manufacturers, who in turn raise prices again. Unless they are controlled by outside forces, prices can soar to the hyperinflation stage, such as in Germany between the two World Wars. In the case of the dot.com bubble of the late 1990s, the desire for Internet-related stocks sparked higher stock prices, which in turn fueled demand, since speculators believed that there was a growing market for Internet commodities. The escalating demand only caused prices to soar even further—and the bubble was on its way to bursting. As was the case in Germany with hyperinflation, the dot.com bubble came to an end with disastrous consequences for speculators.

It may seem odd to place schools in the same discussion as weeds and Internet stocks. But, over the past two decades, education has

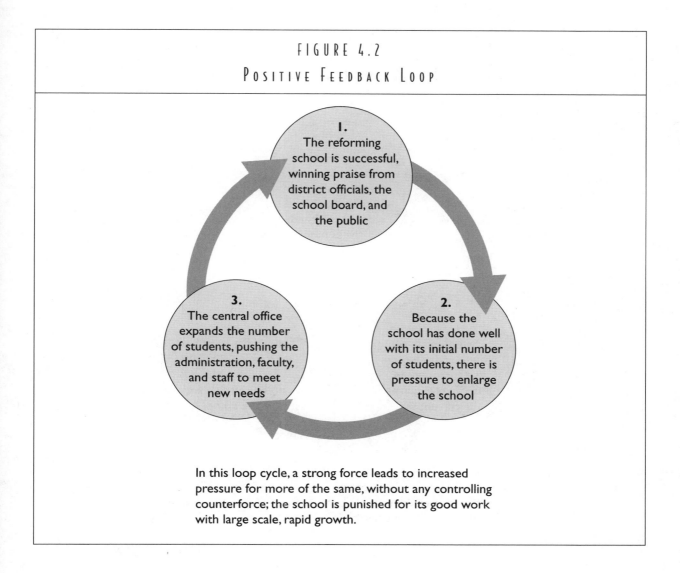

FIGURE 4.2
POSITIVE FEEDBACK LOOP

1.
The reforming school is successful, winning praise from district officials, the school board, and the public

2.
Because the school has done well with its initial number of students, there is pressure to enlarge the school

3.
The central office expands the number of students, pushing the administration, faculty, and staff to meet new needs

In this loop cycle, a strong force leads to increased pressure for more of the same, without any controlling counterforce; the school is punished for its good work with large scale, rapid growth.

moved from the periphery to the center of many discussions—a concentration that has led some noneducators to reduce our institutions to mere commodities. In order to counter these forces, it is incumbent on innovating schools and their allies to understand how overly rapid growth works.

A school's very success can place it at risk for a positive feedback loop. Many reforming schools start in areas not known for high student achievement. Then a reforming school gives students the opportunity to learn in new, more effective ways. Over the first few years, perhaps test scores start to rise, or perhaps there

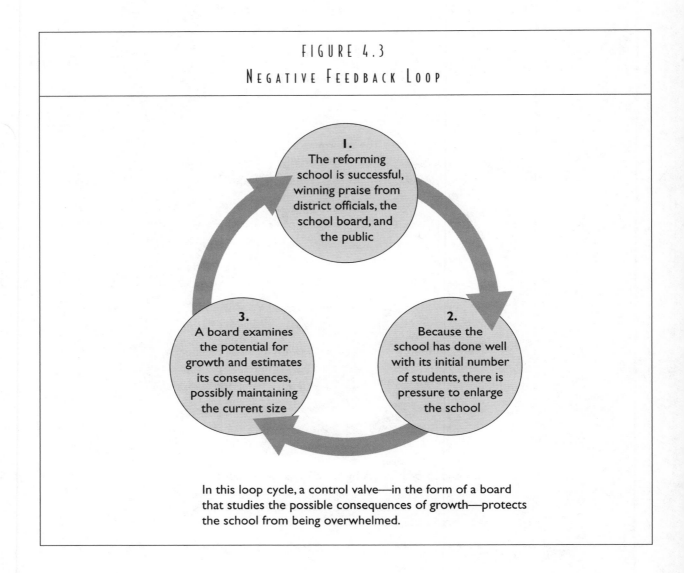

FIGURE 4.3
NEGATIVE FEEDBACK LOOP

1.
The reforming school is successful, winning praise from district officials, the school board, and the public

2.
Because the school has done well with its initial number of students, there is pressure to enlarge the school

3.
A board examines the potential for growth and estimates its consequences, possibly maintaining the current size

In this loop cycle, a control valve—in the form of a board that studies the possible consequences of growth—protects the school from being overwhelmed.

are other indicators of meaningful gains in student learning. Soon district officials notice these improvements and start to make assumptions about possible growth. While their motivation may not be clear, their desire to capitalize on success is: If the school does well with 500 students, why not spread the benefits to 800? If the plan works well for grades K–6, why not expand it to grades 7 and 8? Perhaps there is pressure on the district to show that its schools can innovate on a larger scale, which might mean replicating the approach in neighboring schools throughout the district.

The pressure for growth is an important ingredient in the positive feedback loop, but alone it is not enough to cause chaos. The sincere efforts of the reforming school's staff, faculty, and principal to accommodate the new numbers and somehow make this new configuration work might actually make conditions even worse. This can be readily imagined. New levels of growth are dictated by the central office. The school scrambles to comply, and does at first. The central office sees this and concludes that there is more room for more students, since there was success with the first stage of growth. Perhaps there is a decision that the reforming school has far greater capacity for growth than anyone imagined. The next wave follows, and so on, until the school is overburdened. Even if everyone were acting in good faith, the fallout from this positive feedback loop is clearly devastating to those wishing to sustain innovation. What can be done?

One clear problem with the feedback loop at Bodsworth is that there was no self-correcting mechanism in place. Forces grew stronger and stronger until they were out of control. Though the movement for growth eventually died down, the reforming school, like the tree overwhelmed by an invading vine, was taken down with it. Like the tree, the school had no defense against this force.

A Crucial Corrective: The Negative Feedback Loop

The self-correcting mechanism is a hallmark of negative feedback loops, which we use all the time in our daily lives. The family that reviews its monthly spending and decides to trim some costs to stay on budget, for example, is using a negative feedback loop. The monthly review keeps spending from lurching out of control, since an unchecked desire for more and more things could otherwise become a positive feedback loop that threatens the family's finances.

Nature also develops defenses to check new threats: The vine described earlier may have grown unchecked in New England, but had natural enemies in its original country. Cars equipped with all-wheel drive use the same logic. When a wheel starts to spin out of control in the snow, the car's computer senses this and shifts power to the gripping wheels until the car is stabilized. The driver does not have to think through this process—it is built into the system.

Using Positive and Negative Feedback Loops

If nature provides its own negative feedback loops, and if we can design them for use in cars, why can't we do the same in our schools? In fact, we already do in many instances. One good example is the use of effective instructional supervision. Using best practices, administrators and lead faculty give teachers clear feedback, supportive coaching, focused professional development, and a reasonable plan for continued growth. Without this kind of instructional supervision, a positive feedback loop can easily be imagined, where weak teachers work in isolation and develop ineffective habits that only mount with time, leading to poor results for learners.

Note that the negative feedback loop in Figure 4.3 is multifaceted, and unlike the positive feedback loop, contains a crucial control point. In the context of the problem with rapid growth, a negative feedback loop can be constructed to hold growth to a reasonable size.

Instead of dictating the desired degree of growth to schools, district officials should conduct dialogues with stakeholders to create an effective balancing mechanism. When administrators, teachers, parents, and students hold organized discussions with district leaders, the results seem far less likely to derail a school's work, particularly if the district officials strive to answer any fiscal and equity questions that might help create reasonable growth expectations and avoid an us-versus-them mentality. At the very least, such dialogues will result in more people gathering and analyzing data, leading to more accurate and logical decisions. This way, a self-correcting mechanism is put into place and the negative feedback loop is established.

Building a Negative Feedback Loop through a Growth Analysis Team

If your school is to have a negative feedback loop to respond to the pressure of overly rapid growth, you may wish to consider implementing a Growth Analysis Team (GAT). The purpose of a GAT is to bring more voices into the decision-making process, make sure that growth is congruent with a school's innovations and unique needs and strengths, and help schools synchronize their plans with others in the district so that they are not isolated.

The first step in creating a GAT is designing the team's composition. All of the school's stakeholders need to be represented in the GAT, including faculty, staff, parents, building administrators, district officials, and school board members. Students should participate too, in capacities tailored to their ages and abilities. The team should have about 14 members; more than 20 members may not be practical, and small groups of five or fewer can suffer from overload and not enough differing points of view. Because team members will be required to skillfully collect and analyze data, a consultant with experience in this area may be needed unless such expertise already exists in the system.

Because the school board and superintendent bear ultimate responsibility for a school's success, it makes sense for the GAT to report to them. This means that the board and superintendent need to initiate the GAT's work carefully. Beyond anything else, the team members must understand that their results will be taken seriously. The charge and the timing of GAT results need to be fashioned in such a way as to fit school cycles. The board should provide the team with a clear timeline for results and a set of guiding questions that can serve as a starting point.

The type of data to be collected should be decided upon in advance. What information will help the GAT make recommendations about school growth? Where might the data come from? Local, regional, and even national trends in size and per-pupil costs certainly make sense, but there is more to it: What do important groups in the school and community think of the school's current size? What do they think about the possibility of a larger size? How might they accommodate growth, and what resources might they need to expand reforms effectively and efficiently? The GAT should carefully study the school's curriculum-instruction-assessment dynamics to ensure that any change in school size does not interrupt the reform process.

Once data are gathered from all sources, the GAT needs a strategy for analyzing the information before reporting to the board. What patterns have emerged? How confident is the GAT that these patterns are important and will be sustained over time? What counterarguments are worth considering?

The structure of the GAT report should be considered early on in the process. If the GAT is to really function as a negative feedback loop mechanism, then the team needs to become a routine element of the district rather than an unbearable burden. Recommendations for growth should be tentative, allowing for the possibility of midcourse corrections based on new information or conditions.

In all cases, the point of the GAT is to determine the school's capacity to grow in reasonable ways while still retaining the integrity of its reform design. If the GAT concludes that the school has a limited capacity for growth but pressures for growth persist, then administration, staff, and board members have a serious ethical dilemma to confront. Should they give in to pressure, even though this may harm the school's reform, or should they resist and risk the animosity of community members? This is not a time for despair, but a time to fill the political environment with as much dependable data as possible. Thoughtful information, shared calmly with many interest groups, may open up pathways heretofore closed to reason.

5
Understanding Rising Expectations

HOW SHOULD SCHOOLS RESPOND TO THEIR OWN SUCCESS WHEN IT LEADS to ever-increasing expectations that they one day will not be able to meet? Like growth itself, the capacity of innovating schools is seen as elastic. But whereas growth can be easily seen, rising expectations show themselves in more subtle ways.

Unlike growth, expectations are not dictated by the central office. Of course, there are currently many standards linked to high stakes tests in almost all of our schools, and the expectations embedded in these standards have a powerful effect on learning, despite being designed far from the schoolroom doors. But standards are not the only ways that expectations are created. New members of a school community may be shocked at what passes for success at innovative schools, and may even see the reforms as antithetical to their own values; in such cases, expectations are going to change drastically.

The expectations of everyone who works at the school will change as their jobs change during the reform process. Staff members who used to have well-defined jobs within a secure structure may now find that in addition to their routine work, they are expected to take responsibility for sustaining comprehensive reform by taking part in teams or committees composed of teachers and administrators as well as other staff colleagues. In my discussions with staff members at innovating schools, few complained about having a voice on large issues, and many were active contributors. While the benefits of their participation far outweighed the costs, there were additional time demands placed on many of them.

For faculty, the rise in expectations tied to reform can be seen in more committee meetings, ambitious professional development programs, and teams for delivering new curriculum effectively. Of course, participation in these activities is in addition to the day-to-day routines of lesson planning, teaching, and after-class work. Emotional pressure can create expectations as well: When teachers join in launching a new reform venture they are making a commitment, one price of which is having to evaluate the school's welfare in very personal terms. In my conversations with teachers, they spoke about the reform efforts as they would about their own families, whether things were going well or not. As with the staff members who were pleased with their newfound influence, these teachers appreciated being able to help guide reforms. Still, it was easy to see the worry on their faces when they spoke about serious challenges ahead.

Teachers in the reforming schools I studied did not feel that their efforts were wasted, nor did they resent their administrators. They also did not want the new expectations of joint planning to diminish the attention they paid to students.

Principals share many of the same pressures as staff members and teachers, and have a few unique expectations of their own. Their schools need to run efficiently and obey district rules, but must also be true to their mission. Principals are the chief spokespersons for their schools at the district level, such as at meetings of the superintendent's cabinet; as such, they must be able to defend school practices that may seem unusual or even troubling to colleagues in other buildings. In one case, a magazine article about a reforming school I researched led principals in other district schools to react with jealousy at superintendent's meetings.

On a more concrete level, principals of innovating schools need to understand and be able to justify resource requirements that may differ from those at more traditional schools in the district. For example, principals who use detailed portfolios as assessment tools must be able to defend expenditures associated with such a system. What will other principals say when they ask for additional funds to train teachers in evaluating portfolios? If the school uses grant monies for such purposes, how will the principal find release time for staff and faculty to do well on site visitations and maintain the grant? While the principals I spoke with were pleased to be running schools that dared to experiment, and were able to sustain their promising new practices, they also admitted that the workload was very high and that additional support staff was often lacking due to inadequate funding.

All members of the school communities I studied shared additional pressures as a result of their reform efforts that amounted to increased expectations. For instance, many noted that their districts found their reform programs acceptable just as long as student test scores did not decline. To ensure that this happened, many efforts were made to align innovative practices with district and state standards. However, this raised the following questions:

- What happens if the alignment process moves a school away from the kind of curriculum-instruction-assessment that it believes in?
- If the price of continuing reform is scoring well on tests designed to measure the progress of someone else's curriculum, isn't that asking the school to turn its back on its own learning agenda?
- When officials require continued success on tests that may not be relevant to the school, what does this say about their understanding of the reform, and their courage in helping nurture serious change in the face of possible criticism?

Reforming schools need to exist in two worlds and perform well in both: the world of traditional district expectations and the world of the school's reform model. Is the reforming school well understood and appreciated in the district, or is it an isolated case operating outside of the system? Reform schools often adhere to separate philosophies from others in the district and forge alliances with sponsoring organizations located far away. Teachers in these schools may feel a stronger connection with colleagues who share these alliances than with those in their own district schools.

Looked at in this way, rising expectations are tied not only to students' academic outcomes, but also to the relationships among all at the school. How fair these expectations are may be subject to debate; after all, there must be a price for the freedom to try something new. But it is reasonable for us to wonder just how much staff members, teachers, and principals can do to respond to such diverse and intense pressures to perform.

Action Strategy: Single- and Double-Loop Thinking

One of the elementary schools I studied had such a successful reform program that it suddenly found itself with a requirement to accept and work effectively with middle-school–aged students. This was in spite of the fact that the school's curriculum was designed exclusively for elementary grades. In this case, one remedy would have been to design a negative feedback loop mechanism, such as a GAT. Those interested in helping reforming schools to sustain their course should have an expanding repertoire. This brings us to the concept of single- and double-loop thinking.

Single-Loop Thinking

In single-loop thinking, organizations engage in a three-step process (see Figure 5.1). First, there is an analysis of the current state. Second, after gathering information on current conditions, a comparison is made with accepted standards to see if there is a

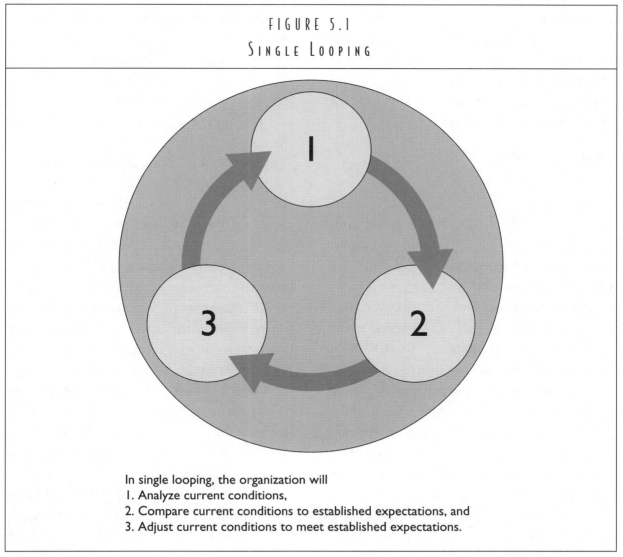

FIGURE 5.1
SINGLE LOOPING

In single looping, the organization will
1. Analyze current conditions,
2. Compare current conditions to established expectations, and
3. Adjust current conditions to meet established expectations.

Note: Adapted from Morgan, G. (1997). *Images of organization* (p. 87). Thousand Oaks, CA: Sage Publications. Copyright © 1997 by Sage Publications. Reprinted by permission of Sage Publications.

difference. Finally, adjustments are made so that standards are met.

Getting your car inspected is a good example of single-loop thinking in action. Your car's pollution control device is monitored, the results are compared to legal standards in your state, and corrections are made if the device is not up to those standards. Little is made of this operation, and there is no discussion about what to do since you and your repair shop are operating within a closed system and have no real choice.

Double-Loop Thinking

Now imagine that you're worried about the amount of pollution you're adding to the air each time you start your car. You take your car to the shop for inspection and find that it passes the state's requirement. This time, you and the mechanic start discussing your environmental concerns, and you find out that there is a new device that can be added to the engine to reduce its polluting effects without harming performance. You ask the mechanic to install this device, and drive away feeling socially responsible. By stepping outside of the normal inspection and correction cycle, questioning the norms, and making changes that are appropriate for you, you have moved from single to double looping (see Figure 5.2).

Here is another example of double-loop thinking in action: A principal would like to help new teachers improve their instructional skills, so she studies a variety of new skill-building methods that are tied to district and state standards and proven effective. All fall she works with a small group of first-year teachers, measuring their teaching with an instrument that is widely used in her state. The process is simple: The principal notes a teacher's actions on a checklist, and at the end of the observation shows the teacher where the lesson met expectations on the checklist and where it did not. They then discuss corrective actions for the future.

It all seems so simple, and a fine case of single-loop thinking, but there is a problem. The observation checklist doesn't introduce the new methods that the principal wants to share, nor does it allow for demonstrating the growth of these methods over time. Though the instrument could be used repeatedly to provide snapshots of teacher performance, it is otherwise not a very good indicator of sustained teacher work. The more the principal thinks about it, the more the inadequacies of the instrument start to outweigh the benefits. She decides to discuss this problem at length both with her staff and with the professional development staff in the central office. A new feedback system is discovered at a reforming school nearby. The new system includes videotaping, debriefing protocols for principals, and a much better aligned checklist. Using the new system, the principal's school becomes a center for a different kind of supervision, evaluation, and professional development. This new process is the direct result of double looping: The

FIGURE 5.2
DOUBLE LOOPING

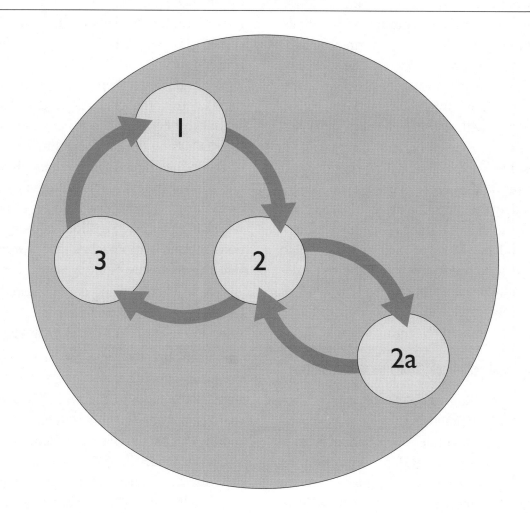

In double looping, the organization will
1. Consider current conditions,
2. Compare current conditions to established expectations,
2a. Take a step back to consider the validity of those expectations, and
3. Adjust behaviors accordingly.

premise of the old system is questioned, leading to an entirely new process.

Two things stand out in both of these double-loop thinking examples. First, single-loop thinking tends to be the norm: The habits that take us through the day often serve us well, and we cannot constantly question everything or we might lose all perspective. Second, we will at times develop new perspectives, often resulting from new knowledge and new experiences. This occurs when the traditional way of working no longer seems adequate. Both the driver and the principal in the examples above had arrived at a richer understanding of their actions, which led to serious questions about the old rules and, finally, a new approach. This kind of switch from single- to double-loop thinking can be used to help reforming schools.

Applying Single and Double Looping in Your Setting

Although reforming schools can be laboratories for new practice, they are not excused from the responsibilities every school faces— namely, welcoming students and helping them to learn effectively. This places a strain on the faculty and leadership of an innovative school that does not exist in traditional schools. In single-loop thinking, we expect that everyone at a reforming school will build a new educational system in addition to completing their regular duties. Their work will be measured in traditional ways, and they will be rewarded or punished accordingly.

Yet it seems unfair to expect so much extra effort from one school but not from others in the district. This may create a disincentive to reform at a time when change should be welcomed. But what if there is no widespread understanding of the reforming school's work? And what if there is no appreciation for the fact that the changes at the reforming school can be spread to other schools in the district? Using double-loop thinking, we can question the original system that tells teachers and administrators in reforming schools to do everything everyone else does on top of their reforming process. The door is then open to construct new approaches that will facilitate reform and ensure equity.

A first step to using double-loop thinking to modify rising expectations is the Reform Effort Energy List (REEL) shown in Figure 5.3.

Begin by creating a list that reflects the pressures of rising expectations. The first column of the table in Figure 5.3 shows items that I found at reforming schools. You should modify this list to reflect your school's specific situation. Once these have been set for your school, start collecting baseline data. This means recording the current time commitments of you and your staff. Be sure to record the work of noninstructional staff as well as faculty. Next, make a fair estimate of the time similarly invested in traditional schools in your area. This will allow you to make a reasonable comparison and help to determine the extra work to be done at your school.

FIGURE 5.3

THE REFORM EFFORT ENERGY LIST (REEL)

Source of Reform Effort	Current Time Devoted by Noninstructional Staff	Current Time Devoted by Teaching Faculty	Current Time Devoted by Administration	Time Devoted by Comparison Noninstructional Staff	Time Devoted by Comparison Teaching Faculty	Time Devoted by Comparison Administration	Time Difference Between Your School and Comparison School
Increased time meeting with parents and community members							
Committee planning work							
Curriculum-Instruction-Assessment work at grade level or in high school departments							
Curriculum-Instruction-Assessment work that cuts across grades or high school departments							

(continued)

FIGURE 5.3 (CONTINUED)

THE REFORM EFFORT ENERGY LIST (REEL)

Source of Reform Effort	Current Time Devoted by Noninstructional Staff	Current Time Devoted by Teaching Faculty	Current Time Devoted by Administration	Time Devoted by Comparison Noninstructional Staff	Time Devoted by Comparison Teaching Faculty	Time Devoted by Comparison Administration	Time Difference Between Your School and Comparison School
Measuring the need for new resources and pursuing grants from governmental sources, corporations, or foundations							
Effectively using new resources and tracking and reporting to funding agencies							
Planning for field visits from funding agencies and responding to their requirements							

(continued)

FIGURE 5.3 (CONTINUED)
THE REFORM EFFORT ENERGY LIST (REEL)

Source of Reform Effort	Current Time Devoted by Noninstructional Staff	Current Time Devoted by Teaching Faculty	Current Time Devoted by Administration	Time Devoted by Comparison Noninstructional Staff	Time Devoted by Comparison Teaching Faculty	Time Devoted by Comparison Administration	Time Difference Between Your School and Comparison School
Representing and defending the school and its reform to the outside world (e.g, in district and school board meetings)							
Engaging in specialized training and professional development (e.g, traveling and sharing at conferences)							

Once these steps have been completed, the REEL inventory needs to be updated annually in all categories. The results can be quantified, measured, and compared objectively to allow your leadership team to keep a record of the change in activities over time. From here you can build a self-regulating process to answer such questions as, "Why are we working more now on reform than we did at this time last year?" Individuals can even develop their own REEL profiles. Without becoming overly bureaucratic, this process can help leaders see where people may be close to burning themselves out. The point of the REEL inventory is to move the reform discussion from a nebulous and debilitating anxiety over rising expectations toward action. Educators using instruments like REEL can enter into discussions with district leaders armed with evidence to guide their thinking.

The extent to which educators and staff at reforming schools put more time into their work than do personnel at traditional schools can add up to greater expectations of the reformers. By sharing the findings in the REEL inventory, reforming leaders can help all decision-makers understand how much work they are actually doing and why single-loop thinking will not do. Educators can use the REEL data to ensure a more equitable set of time expectations.

The REEL concept is only a first step to deconstructing the problem of rising expectations. From this very concrete inventory, a more subtle conversation can begin dealing with the pressures felt by staff, teachers, and administration at the reforming school. The wise district administrator will see the innovating school less as a quirky part of the district, and more as an exciting place to understand new educational directions from which all can learn.

Shared Governance as a Crucial Democratic Forum

6

HOWEVER IMPORTANT THE RESPONSES TO RAPID GROWTH AND RISING expectations are, they are not enough to keep the innovating school true to its mission. The concept of shared governance is central to the continuing work of the schools that I have researched. Although there is some variation from school to school, they also share a great many characteristics.

Seven Qualities of Effective Shared Governance

Whether at the elementary, middle, or high school level, shared government plans have seven important common qualities (see Figure 6.1):

1. Responsibilities tied directly to reform. Shared government only exists where there are serious responsibilities tied directly to the reform agenda. In the schools I studied, representatives of each school community were asked to think through current reform issues and plan for new challenges or areas of growth. For instance, one high school used shared governance to develop its freshman and sophomore house concept. By making this an agenda item for shared government, the school moved away from an ad hoc to a more continuous and planned form of development.

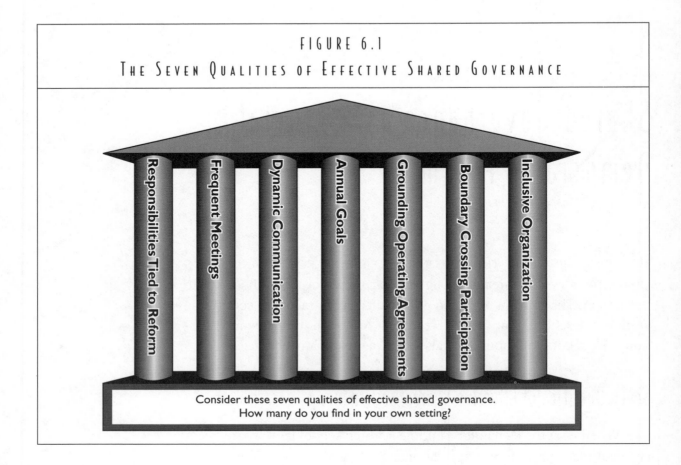

FIGURE 6.1
THE SEVEN QUALITIES OF EFFECTIVE SHARED GOVERNANCE

Responsibilities Tied to Reform

Frequent Meetings

Dynamic Communication

Annual Goals

Grounding Operating Agreements

Boundary Crossing Participation

Inclusive Organization

Consider these seven qualities of effective shared governance.
How many do you find in your own setting?

2. Frequent meetings. Meeting often makes perfect sense when you consider how responsible these bodies are in the development of new projects and sustaining current ones. At the schools I studied, people knew that participating in shared governance would take up a lot of their free time and still agreed to become involved. Terms of office were limited so that teachers did not forsake their futures. Frequent meetings were required at one school that needed to develop a self-study for a site visit from a funding agency. This meant that the work for the self-study was more evenly shared among more people; in addition, the meetings helped those involved develop a greater understanding of one another as individuals. Scheduling meetings frequently is a good way to establish familiarity.

3. Dynamic communication. Although you and others in a small group may have discussed many important issues, the rest of the group may still have little or no idea of what is going on. In this type of situation, governing bodies run the risk of moving far ahead of their constituencies, which can lead to misunderstandings, even in relatively tranquil times. In times of high stress, this can undermine the immense level of trust necessary to keep reform moving forward. The shared governance systems I studied held many meetings with constituent groups. School-level representatives normally reported back to constituencies at grade-level meetings. Dialogues at these levels can raise new ideas, bring out serious reservations, and allow ideas from the top to be field-tested before commitments are made.

We often hear the term "buy-in." While I find this a rather manipulative concept, at its best it means agreeing to become involved and stay close to the process of change. If we really expect citizens of a school to buy in, the least we can do is respect them by constantly communicating with them.

4. Annual goals.

Highly valued and authentic learning goals must be used as demarcation points throughout the reform process, and a reasonable agenda for action should be set each year. (How these get established is a matter of leadership practiced by the shared governance team in league with the principal. Some of these goals are influenced by forces outside of the school or the district; we will consider these in Challenge 4.) It is crucial that this agenda be shared and seen as a top priority by the vast majority of the school community, or else it is just someone else's agenda. At schools with highly functioning shared governance, it is possible to ask almost anyone about the school's goals for the year and get very similar responses. A typical goal might be, "We need to make sure that the curriculum connections between math and science are made more clear this year." Goals should be specific, measurable, and legitimate in the eyes of the school community.

5. Frameworks or constitutions.

High quality work conducted in an open and engaging way is part of the common picture among reforming schools. One way these schools stay centered is through a clear decision-making process based on a well-defined constitution known to everyone.[1] Although this evolving document is the central framework from which the life of the organization flows, it is a mistake to think that every eventuality should be anticipated when drafting a constitution. A reasonable, well-accepted basis for

---

1 Though it might seem strange to think of a school constitution, it is really a matter of writing down the values of an organization. After all, the constitutions of countries such as the United States, Japan, and India are the basis for everything else that the governments in those countries do. Still, it is important to distinguish between a constitution and all that flows from it; in the case of the United States, the constitution first written in 1787 has been amended 26 times and interpreted constantly through court decisions.

arriving at decisions and an equally reasonable process for changing the framework itself are needed. Reflecting back to Chapter 5, schools need an effective single loop that allows for a smooth process, and a double loop that allows the process itself to change when necessary.

6. Wide, boundary-crossing participation. One way that shared governance starts is with grade-level representation in elementary schools or departmental representation in middle or high schools. The downside of this pattern is that it reinforces divisions just when reforming schools need to think in flexible, holistic ways. For instance, if an elementary school wants to break down the barriers between early and upper grades, teachers from these grades need to work together and learn to understand one another's perspectives. Some tasks, such as detailed curriculum adjustments, do depend upon grade-level expertise, but these are qualitatively different from the decision-making of shared governance groups.

7. Inclusive organizing. Crossing grade-level or departmental boundaries creates a sense of the community and helps shared governance groups think in broader, non-competitive ways. But teachers are not the only people in our schools, and inclusion is not just a superficial nicety, but a deep value. Bringing staff, students, parents, and community members into the decision-making circle helps bring different perspectives together, including those of everyone likely to be affected by a decision. A new requirement of community service prior to graduation, for instance, has a much better chance of being crafted in a reasonable and acceptable way when students and community members are involved. Inclusive organizing helps high-quality shared governance systems transcend lukewarm compliance and move toward enthusiastic action.

The questions in Figure 6.2 will help you assess your own school's performance in each of these seven areas.

Action Strategy: The Steering Committee Meeting

The seven principles of effective shared governance are meant to give you a feeling for the larger picture. From these you can see what it takes to start and sustain an authentic process of power-sharing and democratic decision-making. But what does the process look like as it unfolds? To help you understand the flow of events, I will now detail an actual shared governance steering committee meeting that I attended at a school well practiced in them.

The meeting was held near the end of the school year, just at the time when its revered principal and many of its teachers were preparing to retire. Clearly, the school's

FIGURE 6.2
APPLYING SHARED GOVERNANCE PRINCIPLES TO YOUR SCHOOL

Shared Governance Principle	Questions to Ask
Responsibilities tied directly to reform	What alignment is there between the priorities of your shared governance group and your reform's agenda?
Frequent meetings	Does your shared governance group meet at least twice a month? Are meetings open to a wide group, or just to an "in-crowd"?
Dynamic communication	Who sets the agenda of meetings? How are the concerns of the whole school communicated? How does communication flow from the shared governance group to the wider community? What opportunities are there for dialogue?
Annual goals	Are there reasonable shared goals for the school year? Are these clear enough to be measured?
Frameworks or constitutions	What constitution guides your shared governance process? How might processes be amended? Does this framework have the support of the wider community and is it understood at the district level?
Wide, boundary-crossing participation	To what extent is your process organized to cut across grade levels or departments so that more people from diverse backgrounds can work on issues together?
Inclusive organizing	Are staff members, students, parents, and community members at the shared governance table?

professional community was about to change in very substantial ways. In addition, new high-stakes tests were being used in the district that would possibly challenge the school's long-cherished ability to steer its own course.

The goal of the steering committee meeting was to consider all of the key issues facing the faculty and staff at this crossroads in the

school's life and organize them, so that there could be an effective discussion and decision-making process when the whole school met. Eight people attended the meeting:

- The steering committee chair, a lead teacher well versed in the school's reforms and a long-time member of innovative projects;

- The school principal, whose leadership had brought the school great respect, and on whose watch the current innovations, including the shared governance model, had been established. Though he was unquestionably the school's leader, he acted more as a highly engaged participant than as a director; and

- Representatives from smaller groups. At this school, governance was organized so that teachers from different grade levels met in small subgroups with staff members; a subgroup might include a 3rd grade teacher, a 6th grade teacher, a kindergarten teacher, a bus driver, a custodian, and a cafeteria worker.

During the meeting, the group's focus ranged from very specific issues (e.g., how long teachers could fairly be asked to be on after-school bus duty) to broader ones (e.g., setting goals for the upcoming year). The meeting lasted for about one and a half hours, and was held after school. Careful minutes were kept of each discussion point.

The committee chair acted as a skilled facilitator helping to keep the discussions focused. She never pushed people through topics faster than they wanted to go, and the time allotted for the eight members to share their perspectives seemed sufficient for everyone to be heard and achieve consensus on the issues. I was interested to see that the same careful attention was paid to the bus duty question as to the setting of annual goals. Naturally, members could distinguish between these and knew that annual goals were far more important, but every issue received sincere consideration. It was also clear that the group never lost sight of its mission: to clarify the agenda for the schoolwide meeting and frame questions so that the larger group could work through problems effectively and not become bogged down.

Among the highlights of the meeting was the group's good judgment in deciding to postpone annual goal setting until the start of the new school year. This was a tradition at the school, and by waiting for the new principal to arrive and settle in, the faculty and staff could show respect for their new leader. A less confident group might have become defensive and set goals before the new principal's arrival, thus presenting him or her with a fait accompli.

The group held a constructive discussion on how to work through the annual goal-setting process. The need to include all stakeholders was the first issue mentioned; this was a well-recognized part of the school's culture. Next they listed the raw materials necessary for goal setting, concluding that results from a community survey and student test scores would have to be scrutinized, and that goals would have to reflect district plans leading to new directions for the school. Finally, the group described the process of getting input from all individuals and groups at the school. The end result would be a plan that brought the new principal, new teachers, and staff into the decision-making process, which would itself reflect the results of data about the community, student performance, and district initiatives. The establishment of this plan was one very clear way in which shared governance helped the school to continue on its mission, even during a period of sustained, turbulent change.

Following this discussion, the steering committee engaged in double looping by considering its own role in the larger picture. The goal-setting discussion served as an effective example of single-loop thinking. But by stepping back to wonder about their role amid the swirling forces surrounding them, the committee members showed a deeper understanding of how to sustain the process of innovation. Without becoming lost in questions, they thought through their role in relation to the new principal, the smaller groups that they each reported to, and the general process of goal setting. How, they asked, could their shared governance model be fine-tuned so that the reform process and the democratic institutions would be relevant in this new era?

While agreeing to wait until fall to set annual goals, the group invented a process that would bring the whole school together for that meeting. With a new principal, new teachers, and a new district climate, the time would be ripe to ask larger questions. What general goals did the school want for students? One committee member suggested that the schoolwide meeting start with pairs discussing core values at the school, build to small-group discussions, and end with schoolwide discussions.

I was impressed by several things at this stage of the meeting. First, this was a school that had made concrete progress for over a decade; at the meeting, committee members evaluated the school's growth in technology, which was a specific annual project that year. Yet the group was sensitive to the cycle of development, knowing when to step back and look at the larger picture. No one had to instruct them on this point—they were simply that sophisticated.

Flowing from this long-range view, the committee knew that the new principal, teachers, and staff members would need to be brought into the school culture in an interactive way. It would be inappropriate and ineffective to force the culture upon them, whereas a rich, general discussion with the new arrivals could reestablish the school community. This process had the added benefit of renewing the commitment of the school's veterans, and provided the school with its best chance to move ahead as a unit instead of being immobilized through factional disputes.

At the end of the meeting, committee members drafted an agenda for the schoolwide meeting and organized decision-making processes for their colleagues.

Your Turn: Applying Shared Governance Ideas Through Simulation

Now that you have seen the guiding principles behind effective shared governance programs, it is your turn to practice. This exercise applies to you whether you and your school are old hands at shared governance or not, and will give you a chance to improve your skills as you work through important issues.

Scenario. You sit on the shared governance steering committee at your school, which is facing many important changes in the near future, and you are having a meeting. It is close to the end of the school year and your principal, who is also on the committee, is about to go on to another position. She has been a highly effective leader and was with all of you from the start of your reform process. Although she could easily do so, she refrains from leading this meeting, deferring to the elected committee chair.

In addition to the issue of leadership succession, your school needs to prepare for five to eight new teachers, two new bus drivers, one new secretary, and a new cafeteria worker. Your school's goal this year focused on mathematics instruction and increasing the role of technology in instruction and assessment. Starting next school year, you will need to merge your own work with new districtwide expectations in the core areas of mathematics, English, science, and social studies, both for your own reasons and because you understand how important these subjects are to the new superintendent of schools.

Roles. One of you will take on the role of the steering committee chair. Another person will act as the departing principal. Five people will act as representatives from smaller groups that include teachers, staff members, and parents. Of these, one should be a kindergarten teacher, two should be 6th and 3rd grade teachers respectively, one should be a special education teacher, and one should represent a parent support group. (If you work at a middle or high school, adjust the roles so that they accurately represent your setting.)

Structure. Your group will meet for 90 minutes. Although the committee chair will start the discussion and act as facilitator, be sure to allow for everyone's ideas and concerns. Members should engage in real dialogue and take care not to overlook any key issues. Keep a record of your ideas throughout.

Objective. By the end of the session, you need to have set a clear agenda and an equally workable process for a schoolwide meeting that is coming up in a week. This means discussing all of the issues, working out a way for colleagues in the larger group to participate effectively, and deciding how all of the issues need to be framed.

When you are finished with this simulation, debrief by asking participants the following questions:

1. How effectively did you get full participation? How might this be improved upon?
2. How far did you get working through the list of issues? Did you get stuck on any? What were the dynamics of that experience?

3. How well did your simulation mix detailed questions with overarching issues?
4. How comfortable was each participant?
5. Did you arrive at a workable agenda for a schoolwide meeting?

For groups that want to improve shared governance skills, I would suggest conducting the practices above with an outside friend of the school (sometimes called a "critical friend").

Conclusion to Challenge 2

Perhaps nothing is more central to the life of the innovating school than its mission, because it provides a sense of direction and purpose. As I spoke with teachers, administrators, and students across North America, it was clear to me that they understood what made their schools special, and used that sense of a collective self to make decisions for the future. Yet there are important challenges to the mission of a reforming school.

The same thoughtfulness that allowed many of these schools to start as small-scale experiments needs to be used again as the schools scale up. To ensure reasoned growth, it is advisable for the schools and their communities to take an active role. My hope is that concepts such as positive and negative feedback loops and Growth Analysis Teams will help you to take control of the threat of overly rapid growth.

Ironically, your school's success may also lead to difficulties in the form of rising expectations. Here, the concept of single-loop thinking and the enhanced perspective of double-loop thinking should help all supporters of reform to grasp the larger situation and raise important questions about assumptions of the way things *have* to be. The Reform Effort Energy List (REEL) will help you document the energy that your school is expending, and should help you protect your school from too many new pressures.

Finally, democratic organizations in the form of shared governance are a wise practice for the reforming school. Through such forums, power and responsibility can be spread to nearly everyone in the school community, and problems can be seen as collective, rather than "us vs. them."

By facing the likely pressures of rapid growth and rising expectations squarely, and by employing the combined wisdom of the community, reforming schools become far more capable of using the energy of moderate turbulence to promote exciting new possibilities, rather than becoming swamped by the unenlightened demands of outside forces.

Challenge 3

Our lives are full of surprises for none of us has followed a specific ambition toward a specific goal. Instead we have learned from interpretations and improvised from the materials that came to hand, reshaping and reinterpreting.

—Mary Catherine Bateson (1989)

Sustaining the Culture of Innovation

FIGURE C-3
TURBULENCE GAUGE FOR CHALLENGE 3

Degree of Turbulence	General Definition	Relevant Scenario
Light	Associated with ongoing issues Little or no disruption to the normal work environment Subtle signs of stress	There is little faculty turnover and predictable student turnover. New teachers and students find a welcome home after a careful selection process and are systematically guided through the culture of the school. Similar processes are in place for new families. Advanced teacher-learners are supported in strategic ways that take their personal development into account.
Moderate	Widespread awareness of the issue and its specific origins	There is continuing faculty turnover and larger-than-expected student growth, and there are many new faces among the staff. New teachers are welcomed, but no agreed-upon processes exist to help them add to and blend with the school's culture. Staff members, students, and parents receive a handbook but little more. There may be an awards ceremony honoring advanced teacher-learners, but not much thought is given to their special talents, development, or unique needs.
Severe	Possibility of large-scale community demonstrations A sense of crisis	There are erratic swings in turnover. Disenchanted senior staff members are ready to leave. There is a generational turnover of faculty and staff. Some superficial screening of new arrivals occurs, but little is assured. A rift between old and new faculty is emerging. Whole new grade levels may be taken on by the school with little or no input from families or staff.
Extreme	Structural damage to the school's reform Collapse of the reform seems likely	New teachers seem to appear with no appreciation of the school and its reform program; they are isolated and left to sink or swim. Only superficial awareness is given to new students, and families are not recognized. Veteran teachers are taken for granted and given no financial or structural professional development support.

Challenge 3

Schools that choose to practice deep reform over extended periods of time have made a decision that changes the lives and professional identities of everyone involved. Most of the teachers I studied for *Staying Centered* had a history of hard work and self-improvement and an outstanding desire to make a long-standing contribution to their schools. There is no question in my mind that professional practice at innovating schools is more demanding, and probably more rewarding, for those who dedicate themselves to reform. The same can be said of students and their families: Students are normally engaged in active learning both alone and in well-focused groups, and parents visit their students' schools regularly, helping with instruction and curriculum development. If the culture at these schools seems busy, focused, and intense, it's because the demands on reforming schools make such an approach necessary.

Yet the culture at reforming schools will change over time as colleagues depart and new faculty and staff members arrive. How should we bring new professionals into the school? If we don't do anything, how can we be sure that innovation will continue? If we press too hard, aren't we simply propagandizing? Many new students and families will come to school each year as well; how can we learn from these new faces and still continue the best of our work?

In this section, I will describe ways that new arrivals can be integrated into the culture of reforming schools. By "integrated" I mean adaption on both sides, not merely adjusting the new members into the school's norms. Time will eventually convert new teachers into veterans. What can innovating schools do to help sustain the interest of these valuable pioneers?

Consult the Turbulence Gauge for Challenge 3 (Figure C-3) to determine your own needs in this crucial area.

7

Integrating New Faculty

THE INNOVATIVE SCHOOL IS NOT A CLOSED SYSTEM BUT AN ORGANIC, CON-stantly changing being living in an equally active world filled with pressures, forces, and opportunities. One hallmark of the changing circumstances of a school is the ebb and flow of the professionals spending part of their careers there. When we think of school culture, we naturally come to the central role of teachers, who work constantly with students, administrators, parents, and each other to connect the ideas of innovation to the difficult realities of life. Without teachers, promising designs would never leave the paper on which they were written. In *Staying Centered,* I wrote about the immensely productive work of innovating teachers. Now we need to consider what happens when new teachers are brought into reforming schools, whether due to growth or faculty turnover.

By integration, I do not mean a simple process of indoctrinating teachers into the expectations of an inflexible school community. That is a repressive model, because it assumes that the school community doesn't learn *from* the new teachers. Schools that continue their reforms over the long run expect and desire to learn a great deal from the new people in their midst, whom they expect will help change their school cultures for the better. From the start, we should expect openness from both schools and new teachers. Figure 7.1 illustrates this point.

Figure 7.1 has four quadrants. In the lower left, a rigid new faculty member finds a home in an equally rigid new school. If both observe similar norms, there may be a match, but that match may have little chance of

FIGURE 7.1
THE OPEN OR RIGID SCHOOL AND FACULTY MATRIX

	School Closed and Rigid	School Open to Learning
New Faculty Open to Learning	**Mismatch.** Teacher may become disenchanted or bend to the norms of the school; she may leave the school, or find outside avenues of expression. Potential for a good teacher-to-school fit is lost.	**Possible match.** Mutual learning occurs: The new teacher informs the process of schoolwide growth while learning from the school.
New Faculty Closed and Rigid	**Possible match.** Teacher and school both observe similar norms, but little chance exists for personal or organizational growth in any sustained direction.	**Mismatch.** After many organized attempts, the teacher may be helped to find a more appropriate school in the same district or elsewhere.

helping the individual or the school to develop in a sustained way. In the upper left, we find a new faculty member open to learning who is now working in a rigid, closed school. The new faculty member will likely change to fit the new school, find a creative outlet for her talents outside of the school, or leave. Here, much potential seems lost. In the lower right quadrant, the rigid faculty member joins a school that is an open learning organization. This likely means a different kind of mismatch leading to serious counseling and an exit from the school. Finally, in the upper right quadrant, we find a match between the faculty member and a school where both are anxious to learn and grow.

At one of the reforming high schools I studied for this book, the principal told me that although the selection process was normally successful, one teacher was very unhappy with the school's philosophy. "Because we work in a district, he has many other choices besides our school and we are in the process of counseling him to find a better fit," he said. This turned out to be a case of a rigid teacher at a school open to learning and change. The issue was not so much one of right versus wrong, but of compatability.

In a different high school thousands of miles away, I met with a first-year math teacher whose excitement and sense of finding a wonderful new professional home were obvious. The spirit of constant learning turned out to be what brought her to the school in the first place: She loved mathematics, but wanted to improve her pedagogical skills, especially at creating effective cooperative groups. Hers was a case of a good fit between a growing organization and a developing professional. The schools I visited that were open to learning tended to successfully focus their own energies.

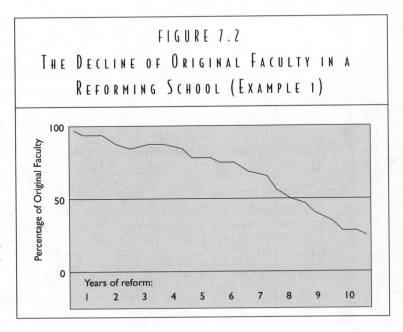

FIGURE 7.2
THE DECLINE OF ORIGINAL FACULTY IN A REFORMING SCHOOL (EXAMPLE 1)

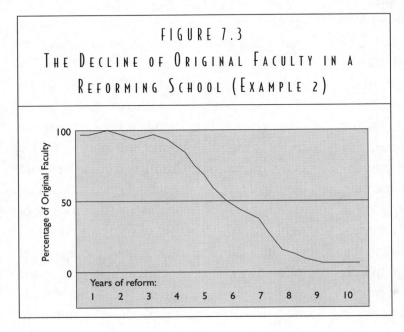

FIGURE 7.3
THE DECLINE OF ORIGINAL FACULTY IN A REFORMING SCHOOL (EXAMPLE 2)

Generational Cycles and the Importance of New Faculty

As with new leaders, new teachers are handed an invaluable trust upon entering a school where important change needs to be nurtured. When a principal departs, nearly everyone is engaged in discussing the transition. This is not always so when teachers depart, yet when even a small number of highly valued teachers leave, their absence casts a shadow on further reforms. Consider the two examples of faculty turnover shown in Figures 7.2 and 7.3.

At the school shown in Figure 7.2, small numbers of teachers began leaving after only the first two years of reform. By the sixth year, about a quarter of the teachers were new, and by the ninth year, over half were new. Clearly, the school would have to make a considerable effort to maintain a supportive and effective culture of development. The effort will have to be even greater for the school in Figure 7.3, with its rapid loss of original faculty and immediate need to bring all new arrivals quickly into the reform process.[1]

Though a steady decline in original faculty is easy to imagine, a more rapid pattern is just as likely. At one school I studied, teachers worked as an energized team for over two decades, sharing skills in what many called a family setting. Eventually, the teachers that began their careers at the school started retiring; at around the same time, one teacher moved away and another left after having a child. Suddenly the school needed to find eight new teachers at once. This presented a challenge to the whole group, because sustaining a positive culture focused on reform was a central priority.

Prehiring Practices

We all know that new teachers don't simply show up at a given school. Even in large districts where teaching posts are assigned, both the teachers and schools normally have a say in the matter. The selection process takes on a special focus and intensity at reforming schools, starting with prehiring practices.

The reputation of a school helps a lot in recruiting. The principals and teachers I talked with spoke of attracting likeminded people, especially those who understood the value of collaboration. Because many of these schools belonged to supportive national organizations, the teachers were connected to a network of peers who knew about their successful practices and with whom they could share news of openings. Such networks are powerful recruiting tools for innovating schools.

Sometimes talented student teachers find employment at their reforming host schools. Among the advantages of this approach is the chance to see the emerging teacher in action and help her learn new techniques; for the candidate, student teaching offers a fair approximation of the amount of work involved at the school, including

---

1 We should remember that loss of faculty does not necessarily mean dramatic problems at the school. Sometimes, teachers leave because their good work has opened up new opportunities at other innovating schools; at other times, they retire. In Challenge 2, I described how schools change the original-to-new teacher ratio simply by adding more students or grade levels.

meetings and professional development pursuits. At one high school I visited, a former student teacher spoke of the strong support he received from a senior teacher, who continued as a valued mentor after the student teacher was hired.

At reforming schools, shared governance bodies have a strong role in the prehiring interview process. Because a school's direction and priorities should be well known and shared among existing faculty, staff, and administrators, a high degree of agreement should exist regarding the kind of talents and abilities that are needed at the school.

Certain general skills always seem appropriate for teacher candidates. These include great initiative, a powerful focus on children, a positive attitude, and a strong work ethic. Underneath these global traits lie a series of specifics. Interviewers were careful to see whether or not the candidate was trained in the particular curriculum-instruction-assessment patterns used in the school. Did the candidate understand a specific science program and its origins (say the American Academy of Science's 2061 report)? Does the teacher bring multiple, compatible methods of instruction? Does the teacher really understand alternative authentic assessment? These probing questions go to the heart of the matter and are in stark contrast to asking whether or not a candidate approves of the reform process at the school. Although new teachers may only have an early understanding, they at least have some grounding and seem much more likely to match the school.

Still, it would be a mistake to think of interviews as one-way cross examinations. At one highly successful elementary school, the principal had a habit of asking candidates about their hobbies. Some cooked, some gardened, others built furniture. This line of questioning gives the school a sense of the candidate as a whole person and opened up new possibilities for blending these avocations into life at the school. The principal also asked the candidates about their visions, both for themselves and for the school, which helped reveal whether or not the teacher and school were compatible. At one urban high school, the principal even went to museums with prospective candidates to better understand them.

Finding the right person for a school so that the culture of creativity can thrive is a subtle endeavor, combining specifics as well as imponderables. This reminds me of an interview I once had with a college president when I myself was looking for work. Things were going well when suddenly her expression became quite serious.

"All right," she asked, "why should we invite you to become a part of our community?"

Luckily, I had thought this one through and spoke forcefully about the values I shared with the college, including a common concern for quality work with students and a sense that the institution and I were both dedicated to a more just society. The college president and I both knew that the school would change my life and that I would have an influence on the school.

Once new teachers are hired they are expected to maintain a positive attitude, as they must work closely together if they are to achieve the ambitious goals of reform. To ensure a positive work environment, teachers should celebrate each others' accomplishments. As one teacher told me, "We will not let a negative person infect the group. If you start to gripe, you will not be encouraged."

Just as important as a positive outlook is mutual understanding, which begins in the interview stage but deepens with the first few days on the job, during which the teacher will learn a great amount about the school's current direction. Sincere questions are asked of the new teacher: What do you know about our reform direction? What do you think of our approach? Asking honest questions helps establish a norm of openness and respect. One administrator told me, "Teachers need to know where we are now, but they also need to know that they are part of us and have the right to have their ideas included. Tradition is good but it is not something you keep just to keep." Reforming schools value loyalty as well as free-spirited connection. As one lead teacher said, "We do this by making new people feel like they belong and that they matter."

Another way of bringing new teachers quickly into the heart of a school is establishing a common policy for sharing data. Transparency is vital: Schools that have sustained reforms make a point of avoiding secrecy and making important information available to anyone needing it. The information loop includes everyone. New hires especially need to know that they are not excluded from the information-sharing process.

One principal made this priority quite plain: "Don't make them feel that they are the last to know. . . . Everybody has equal access to information; I think that is very important."

Many innovating schools have traditions in place that make new teachers feel that they have joined an inclusive organization. One high school conducts a special ceremony at an opening-of-school retreat for teachers and administrators. Everybody joins in a circle, starting with the founding teachers and principal. One by one, they tell the story of the school's reform program and its origins. The story grows naturally, through the voices of those who have spent years bringing the school as far as it has come. Era by era, the twists and turns of the school are shared with new teachers as they prepare to share their ideas and aspirations. In this symbolic ceremony, a new community is formed, flowing from the founders through to the newest arrival. Each year, the work of everyone is honored and sewn into the fabric of the school's narrative. This rich tapestry reflects the school's respect for all who work there, and sends the message that the school's story is evolving along with them.

Two Processes for Supporting New Teachers

Successful reforming schools use direct mentoring and immediate participation in shared governance to help bring new teachers into the community and assure that mutual learning gets off on the right foot. Both approaches require a spirit of flexibility from everyone: New teachers need to be open to learning how to work within the specialized context of an innovating school, and existing faculty and administrators need to show by their actions that they want to learn, too (see Figure 7.4). It is at this stage that the grand talk from interviews either becomes real or fades away as an empty promise.

Direct Mentoring

The practice of mentoring has become widespread over the past half-decade, so the concept is probably not new to you. At the schools I visited, it was common for old hands to eagerly mentor new teachers, whether they were novices or not. At New York City's International High School, new

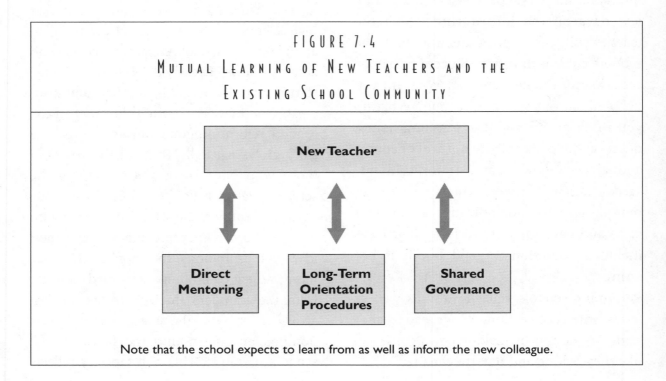

FIGURE 7.4
MUTUAL LEARNING OF NEW TEACHERS AND THE EXISTING SCHOOL COMMUNITY

New Teacher

Direct Mentoring

Long-Term Orientation Procedures

Shared Governance

Note that the school expects to learn from as well as inform the new colleague.

teachers were paired with veterans of the school for a year of team teaching. This approach made it less likely for new teachers to become overburdened, since at least one course preparation was shared with a colleague and helped the novice to learn the routines and cultural features that made the school special.

The two-teacher team is a concrete example of "living the talk" of cooperation and collegial development. At one elementary school I studied, a highly experienced teacher gave a novice one of her best units to use in the classroom. Anyone who has worked with new teachers will recognize what a great gift this was, because it provided the new teacher with effective instructional materials and approaches just when she needed it most. One common principle at reforming schools is that the success of everyone gives all students the best chance of learning. Consequently, narrow competition between teachers is simply not tolerated.

Through direct mentoring, veteran teachers model excellent practice in useful ways to their new colleagues. "His practice of teaching is amazing to me," one teacher told me of her mentor. After lessons, the pair would share thoughts on ways to make them better. This sort of reflection is a serious gain for new teachers, especially at reforming schools, where the first two years of teaching are critically important.

The mentoring relationships at the schools I studied had highly dedicated, well-trained mentors anxious to build long-term relationships with protégés, who for their part wanted to deepen their craft knowledge and share expertise with their more experienced colleagues. You can easily see the contrast between this kind of relationship and those in which both parties simply go through the motions of support and learning without the commitment.

Training Mentors at A. L. Burruss Elementary School

The A. L. Burruss Elementary School in Marietta, Georgia, supports teachers wishing to become mentors through a statewide program called Teacher Support Specialists (TSS). Designed to create a cadre of skilled professional developers from the classroom, TSS educators are expected to do the following:

1. Carry out the roles and responsibilities of TSS teachers and understand the roles of others who supervise teachers;
2. Exhibit effective communication and conferencing skills;
3. Use effective observation and feedback techniques; and
4. Help their protégés to
   - Develop effective and varied teaching skills and techniques; and
   - Develop effective planning skills;
   - Develop techniques to assess the needs, interests, and abilities of learners;

- Use appropriate and varied teaching resources;
- Develop self-assessment skills;
- Develop evaluation techniques;
- Become familiar with local and state curriculum guidelines;
- Comply with accepted professional practices and mature into teachers with high professional and ethical standards; and
- Become reflective about their teaching.

Mentors have a specific code of responsibilities, including:

- Giving information related to procedures, guidelines, and expectations of the school district;
- Collecting, disseminating, or locating materials or other resources;
- Giving information about teaching strategies or the instructional process;
- Offering support by listening empathetically and sharing experiences;
- Giving guidance and ideas related to discipline and student management;
- Offering information about organizing and planning the school day;
- Helping arrange, organize, or analyze the physical setting of the classroom;
- Teaching while the new teacher observes (preceded by a conference to identify the focus of the observation and followed by a conference to analyze the observed teaching episode);
- Critiquing and providing feedback on the beginning teacher's performance to the protégé, not as an evaluation instrument; and
- Giving help or ideas related to conferencing or working with parents. (Georgia Department of Education, 1990)

Training includes shared readings on adult-learning theory, the stages of a teaching career, and effective classroom assessment strategies, through which TSS educators reflect upon their practice. Role-playing is also used. In one situation, the new teacher tells the mentor:

> I work so hard to prepare for classes. I work hours getting ready. I always have interesting activities for my classes. I know that sometimes students forget or things are out of their control but I AM SO FRUSTRATED! I CANNOT GET THEM TO DO THEIR HOMEWORK!!

When responding, the mentor is advised not to engage in a "whine-and-jeez party," but to act as a coach—to help problem-solve rather than commiserate. It takes more than exhortations to move from a fellow complainer to a mature guide, and TSS training is designed to do just that.

Helping veterans to become successful observers of instruction is an obvious area of focus for TSS mentors. During training, they are asked to look carefully for at least six types of patterns in a teacher's questioning technique:

1. How many questions actually requested a student response?
2. Were there poor questioning patterns, such as the use of repetitious phrases, one-word-answer questions, and multiple or wordy questions?
3. What thought levels were demanded in response? (Use Bloom's taxonomy to go beyond merely fact-recall questions.)
4. What is the relationship between the teacher's intentions and the questions asked?
5. What is the relationship between the lesson objectives and the questions asked?
6. What is the relationship between the vocabulary used and the students' verbal abilities?

This level of detail shows the careful and specific professional development given to TSS mentors. In addition, observational skills are linked to effective conferencing practices that help the mentor stay in question-posing rather than master-teacher mode. Brainstorming, probing, and trying out alternative strategies help the new teacher learn to work through problems with colleagues, thus knocking down the dysfunctional notion that asking for help is a sign of incompetence. These approaches also help the school pass along one of its deepest cultural values: that student learning is best assured through the combined work of the whole group, rather than through the work of isolated teachers.

TSS mentors work on their own philosophies of teaching and study the ethical standards expected of teachers. By drawing connections among their core beliefs, teachers find common cause with colleagues and interesting points of philosophical difference. They might even find historic antecedents for their beliefs. In *Staying Centered,* I noted that innovating schools often blend elements of several belief systems, as shown in Figure 7.5. By mapping out their own beliefs and the traditions that they follow, teachers and the entire school community can become more fluent at articulating their ideas and practices.

Naturally, many of the ethics that teachers are taught have to do with state laws. These include reporting abuse, honoring student confidentiality, refraining from inappropriate activities when students are present, and steering clear of any illegal activities.[2]

---

2   But this is only a start. Writers such as Shapiro and Stefkovich (2001) have described an integrated system of ethical models, including the ethics of justice, care, critique, and the profession. These can be used to work through the richly complex questions that can arise from classroom practice. Just like the study of educational philosophy, the pursuit of ethics is a special part of the culture of innovating schools.

Shared Governance

Shared governance is a critical way for innovating schools to work through the challenge of continuous development and bring new people into an organization. At most reforming schools, new teachers immediately join teams for weekly and monthly meetings to discuss school priorities and reflect on individual concerns. These democratic forums are an effective way to empower newcomers, have them participate in decision-making, and show them respect through engagement and trust.

As with the other teacher-integration approaches discussed here, shared governance supports the value of combined work and shared responsibility instead of too much reliance on authority figures. The Otter Valley troika example in Chapter 3 shows how teachers can nurture and sustain reform, and how pivotal their participation is to the long-range goals of serious change.

FIGURE 7.5
CHARACTERISTICS OF FOUR PHILOSOPHIES
THAT GUIDE CURRICULUM LEADERSHIP

Essentialism

Major Elements

- Structure and rigor
- Logical, chronological curriculum
- Emphasis on math and science

Goal: Protect democracy from foreign economic or political threat.

Perennialism

Major Elements

- Universal truths
- Moral and intellectual habits
- Emphasis on liberal arts for all

Goal: Nurture and regenerate democratic habits of mind.

Progressivism

Major Elements

- Respect for individuals
- Investigation/problem solving
- Emphasis on community standards

Goal: Build democracy through experience.

Existentialism

Major Elements

- Emphasis on one's own standards
- Self-structured learning

Goal: Redefine democracy in personal terms.

Action Strategy: The Concept Attainment Model

Schools that sustain innovation tend to make integrating new teachers an interactive process by opening up their school cultures to the newcomers' gifts. This allows for deep renewal instead of heavy-handed and simplistic indoctrination. Each of the processes we considered in this chapter calls for serious decisions by nearly everyone in the community, including district leaders, building administrators, teachers, staff members, and families. Because integrating new faculty means building many new concepts within the school community, I suggest using the Concept Attainment model first described by Bruner, Goodnow, and Austin (1956) and modified later by Gunter, Estes, and Schwab (1999). The model employs an inductive process that normally takes two hours to prepare for and one hour to present to a group. I have taught and used this model for many years, and find that it leads to a deep and sustained understanding of complex ideas. Better than simply relating or even illustrating the subtleties of a concept, the model helps groups to construct their own meaning and discern shades of difference between related but distint concepts.

Because the careful introduction of new teachers (both those new to teaching and veterans) is so important, and since that kind of painstaking work is not the norm in all schools, we need to practice these new steps. I would suggest that each of the practices is really a new concept. Take the work done in prehiring, for example. At Oceana High School and the Burruss Elementary School, this involved serious understanding of the school's curriculum-instruction-assessment development; the central skills, knowledge, and attitudes that would be needed in these areas in the near future; and the hard work and collaborative attitude that a teacher new to the school would need to make a smooth transition.

Though I will demonstrate the process of the concept attainment model here as it applies to prehiring practice, the model may be used for any of the integration processes described in this chapter. The key to concept attainment is that it allows school leaders to explore the heart of a new idea collaboratively with colleagues. Figure 7.6 shows how it works.

Step 1: Determine the Central Qualities of the Concept

Teacher-leaders and administrators should study the details of the concept and define its key attributes. In our case, this means

- Looking carefully at the qualities of prehiring at the innovating schools,
- Understanding the school's mission,

FIGURE 7.6
THE CONCEPT ATTAINMENT MODEL

The Steps of Concept Attainment	As Applied to New Faculty Integration
1. Determine the central qualities of the concept.	Determine what really matters when integrating new faculty.
2. Find clear examples of the concept in action.	Find examples of well-integrated new teachers at the school.
3. Find clear nonexamples of the concept.	Identify cases that have nothing to do with integrating new faculty.
4. Contact the group.	Introduce the process of concept attainment to the group.
5. Provide the group with a "yes" example.	Relate an instance of effective new faculty integration to the group.
6. Provide the group with a second "yes" example.	Reinforce the concept by relating another instance of effective new faculty integration to the group.
7. Provide the group with "no" examples.	Relate two instances of ineffective new faculty integration to the group.
8. Build the concept from its parts.	Ask the group to link information from the "yes" and "no" examples to carefully build a concept.
9. Test out the concept.	Ask the group to identify "yes" and "no" examples without saying which are which.

Note: Adapted from Gunter, M. A., Estes, T. H., & Schwab, J. (1999). *Instruction: A models approach* (3rd ed.). Boston: Allyn and Bacon. Copyright © 1995 by Pearson Education. Adapted by permission of the publisher.

- Asking prospective teachers to share their experiences with specific, relevant instructional techniques,
- Being aware of and perhaps experienced with authentic assessment, and
- Being able to examine standardized tests results.

Of course, interviews are also an attribute of the prehiring process; from the administrator's perspective, this may be described as taking time to get to know the ambitions and talents of a possible new colleague.

Step 2: Find Clear Examples of the Concept in Action

Determining most of the key dimensions of the prehiring process is an advantage, but now you need to find specific examples of the process in action. Perhaps you can find a short video clip that shows a new teacher carefully explaining her approach to instruction, or a focused role-play dealing with the interview process. The form should be varied to keep your audience interested; the key is to help them understand your concept through rich, well-chosen examples.

Step 3: Find Clear Nonexamples of the Concept

One of the strengths of this concept attainment model is the use of non- or "no" examples. These will help you convey what you do and do not mean by the concept. Nonexamples might include working with

others to present a role-play of an unfocused interview where specific leading techniques are never discussed, or presenting a video depicting veteran teachers griping about working conditions to a teacher candidate during an interview.

Step 4: Contact the Group

Introduce the process of concept attainment to your audience—in this case, probably a faculty, parent, or board meeting. Begin by drawing a two-column table, with one column labeled "'yes' examples" and the other labeled "'no' examples." Tell the audience members that you plan to use clear examples to build a concept together with them.

Step 5: Provide the Group with a "Yes" Example

Let's say you begin by showing a video of a new teacher being mentored by a veteran. Ask the group to offer comments about what they have seen and list them in the "yes" examples column of your table. One person might observe that careful attention is paid to the new teacher, another might see an emphasis on instruction, and yet another might see one-on-one work.

Step 6: Provide the Group with a Second "Yes" Example

Suppose your new example is a video of a hiring interview between a candidate and the school's shared governance committee.

You will find that many of the observations made about the first example pertain to this one as well; in both cases, for example, careful attention is paid to the new teacher and emphasis is still placed on instruction, so these items stay on the list of prehiring attributes. However, the interview example differs from the mentoring video in that it doesn't include one-on-one work, so that item is crossed off the list. Following this, ask the group if there are any other observations they would like to add to the "yes" list.

Step 7: Provide the Group with "No" Examples

Offer two "no" examples to help the group see what you *don't* mean by the concept. These may be similar to the "yes" examples, but perhaps in this case the mentoring meeting has no particular focus, or the interview has no clear priorities. In other words, the "no" examples help us to notice the important underlying elements of an ideal prehiring process. Participants might point out poor attention to detail, no sense of the school's mission, no evidence of careful training, or lack of adherence to a thoughtful process.

Step 8: Build the Concept from Its Parts

After you have shown four or five "yes" examples and three or four "no" examples, it is time to shift gears. You will want to ask the audience to look at the "yes" and "no" lists and think carefully about them. Help them to build a definition of the concept together; only then should you give the concept a name. Unlike a traditional lecture, your group members will build the definition together and you can be much more sure that when they leave the room, they will have a shared way of defining the concept with all of its important elements. They will likely also leave with a sense of ownership.

Step 9: Test Out the Concept

Finally, to reinforce the concept, give two new examples, one "yes" and one "no." This way you will be able to see how well your group understands the concept. The "yes" example could be a video of a prospective teacher demonstrating his portfolio of relevant past experience; the "no" example could be a photo of a busy principal rifling through resumes just before an interview. Although I used the prehiring qualities of integrating the new faculty member for this example, you may use concept attainment for any or all of the parts of the program that you want to bring to your school.

Using the Action Strategy of Concept Attainment to Help You Integrate New Faculty

Because bringing new veteran and novice teachers into your school is both inevitable and crucial to your continuing success, I hope that the pattern described in this section will be of interest. You may be using some of these ideas already, such as a mentoring program. It may be, however, that you are not satisfied with the quality or direction of the elements now in place. If this is your situation, use concept attainment to sharpen your program and improve its quality. If you are embarking on new facets of your process, you may want to use concept attainment to sharpen your own understanding by defining all of the key attributes and finding illustrative "yes" and "no" examples. You will also help your audience to explore these as they work through the process with you. In either case, it will be important for you to think through your priorities carefully, and raise the awareness of your group slowly through iterative practices like concept attainment, if you want to build long lasting agreement to change your work with new colleagues.

8

Integrating New Families and Students

ONE THING THAT SETS REFORMING SCHOOLS APART FROM OTHERS IS THEIR ability to deliver on promises and grow along with the new students and families that annually help to redefine their school. This organic process helps the school to continually refresh its sense of purpose and identity. By contrast, consider the school portrayed in the well-known film *Dead Poet's Society* (1989). Anyone familiar with the opening scenes will remember the speech given by the venerable school head. Looking over an assembled throng of parents and their sons, he recalls his school's success in gaining admission for so many graduates to Ivy League colleges, delighting many in the assembly. Then he lowers his gaze and asks the older students to recite the four pillars that support the school's code. From that moment on, *Dead Poet's Society* pits those who would conform to the strong pressures of the school's culture and become its true citizens against those who evolve in different directions and do not fit in.

Such pressures to erase one's own inner voice are diametrically opposed to the dominant theme of reforming schools. These institutions certainly take pride in their missions, and are clear about what they do well. Significantly, the schools that I visited saw themselves as moving towards goals that became clearer and richer with new events, new needs, new students, and new families. Not only did they accept different kinds of students, they relished the opportunity to grow in new directions as a result. These schools shared four traits that were central to their ability to integrate and learn from students and their families: opting in, mutuality, connectedness, and evolution.

Opting In

Because students attending Oceana High School in Pacifica, California, were able to select the school themselves out of several in their district, they and their families had to think through and agree to the school's emphasis on academics in advance. At the Red Cedar independent school in Bristol, Vermont, prospective students spoke with staff and students before making a decision to attend. The International High School at La Guardia Community College in New York City provides prospective students with applications that they must file in order to attend, thus allowing both the students and the school more of a choice within the public system.

When students are allowed to opt into their learning communities, they feel as though they have selected a school rather than landed there by default. At schools that allowed students to select among alternative possibilities such as learning teams, I found a high degree of personal and family responsibility as well. Nothing can guarantee a successful match, of course, but allowing student interests and learning strengths to inform the school-selection process allows student and their families to feel responsible and empowered.

Mutuality

When Oceana High School was scheduled to receive an influx of new students after another school in the district closed, an opportunity arose. Where some schools would have first thought about how the new students might learn to change in order to fit in, the teachers and administrators at Oceana paired new students with present ones to make sure that they learned from one another. They also spent time with the new students' families.

When I asked the principal to explain the school's work in detail, I was struck by her commitment to change: She told me that the new students had a right to change their new school and its culture to reflect their needs.

Being open to listening and changing is what makes reforming schools unique. Sometimes this means an enhanced sensitivity to cultures that are new to the school; at other times, it may mean working with families from underrepresented income levels or with varied aspirations for their children. The principle of mutuality means learning and being willing to invent a new future based on the imaginations and desires of the new community. Because schools, by their very nature, face a constant cycle of new students, this principle seems both logical and appropriate. Clearly, it requires a great deal of confidence and maturity on the part of educators.

Connectedness

Once enrolled, the students at the schools that I studied began to engage the curriculum-instruction-assessment triangle that is at the heart of learning. The three aspects of this triangle are dynamically connected, so that developing any one point means developing the other two as well (see Figure 8.1).

To illustrate the idea, consider a school that is asked to integrate Chinese history into the early grades. This curricular change may mean that teachers need to study the subject and devise new and engaging ways to share the content with students (instruction). At the same time, the teachers will also need to think through relevant ways for students to share their knowledge (assessment). So, a change in the curriculum will also cause changes in both instruction and assessment.[1]

The particular curriculum-instruction-assessment setup at these schools makes for a

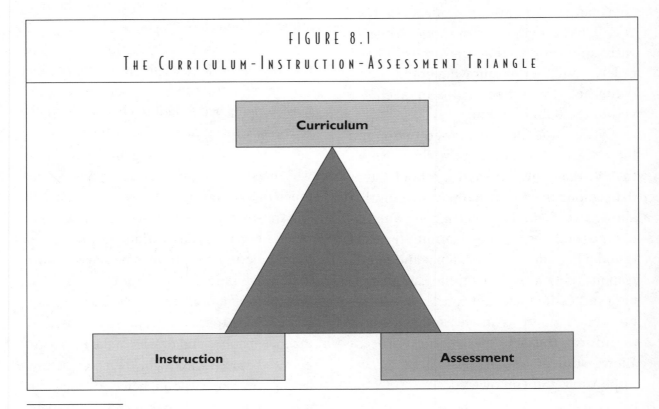

FIGURE 8.1
THE CURRICULUM-INSTRUCTION-ASSESSMENT TRIANGLE

Curriculum

Instruction

Assessment

---

1   The same is true for changes in assessment. As we will see in the final chapter of this book, a change to mandated high-stakes testing from the state level will cause a change in classroom instruction as well as in the learning agenda itself (curriculum).

unique type of openness to new students, as curricular choices often reflect areas of student interest. At one school, decisions about what to study, when, and for how long came from students. Although this may sound like an extreme example, degrees of this kind of openness existed at all the schools I studied. This means that the agenda is not sealed and alien to learners, but rather comes, in part, from them; there is an open door to sharing and investing in the educational process. For example, several of the elementary schools I visited had a particularly balanced approach to language arts because students were allowed to select the books they read.[2]

The curriculum-instruction-assessment triangle opens again when we look at the constructivist instruction that goes on at these schools. At innovating schools, students work in groups, focus on projects, and learn in a hands-on fashion. Passive learning, where students are expected simply to absorb facts, is alien to these schools. The more engaged learners are, the more they help shift the focus away from adult inputs only to a balance of both teacher and student inputs. Clearly, engagement helps bring new students into the heart of the classroom's lifework.

Though reforming schools use traditional tests, they also offer learners many other ways to demonstrate their knowledge and growth over time. Portfolios, student exhibitions, and senior projects were all central to the assessment procedures at the schools I studied, and helped students to personalize their learning experience by making their own priorities a focus of the schoolwide agenda. At one small rural elementary school in Vermont, students learned the core disciplines by constructing gardens, growing food, and selling the vegetables at harvest time. Their hands-on learning and real-world experience gave context and meaning to their learning.

Evolution

The final element that supports the integration of new students and their families is a school's commitment to continuing development (see Figure 8.2). As authentic learning organizations, the schools I visited did not have a rigid goal to achieve, after which they could rest. Continuing success for their students was always the top priority, but the administrators and teachers knew that the concept needed to be continually revisited in a dynamic and turbulent world. This meant that everyone in the schools needed to be part of the process of growth and renewal, not just students or their teachers. The staff at Burruss Elementary School practiced this craft quite

2   As we will see, the current high stakes accountability movement is sometimes viewed as a threat to this freedom.

effectively; regular shared governance meetings involved parents, and strong attempts to engage families were common. Because the question of constant improvement was central, these families not only heard about the school's direction, they had a voice. PTA nights regularly reflected this connection.

By being open to constant learning and invention, innovating schools are thoughtful laboratories for educational change. As such, there tends to be an expectation that every new year brings serious goals involving basic change. Questions about old assumptions in teaching and learning are the norm, again making these schools highly open and dynamic environments. Far from causing instability, committing to the spirit of a learning community typically makes life more secure by opening the concept of invention to nearly everyone and allowing for creative energies to be directed at making the school more successful. Among the beneficiaries are

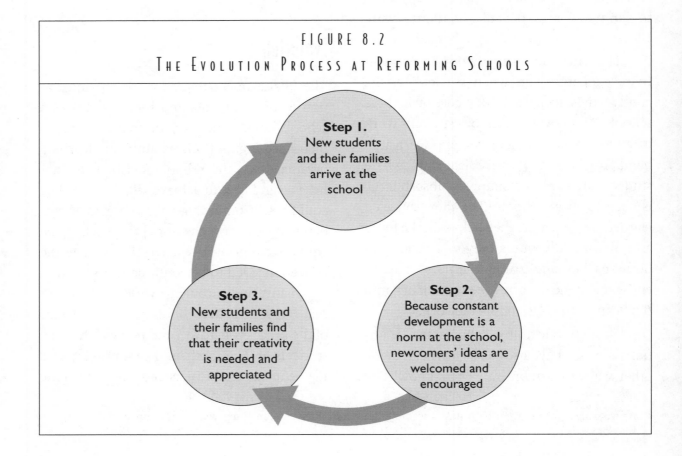

FIGURE 8.2
THE EVOLUTION PROCESS AT REFORMING SCHOOLS

Step 1.
New students and their families arrive at the school

Step 2.
Because constant development is a norm at the school, newcomers' ideas are welcomed and encouraged

Step 3.
New students and their families find that their creativity is needed and appreciated

new students and their families, since the door is open to their talents and ideas. In turn, they are expected to help the school in its latest phase of creation and renewal.

Action Strategy: Scaffolding and the Zone of Proximal Development (ZPD)

Among his many contributions to understanding the learning process, the Russian psychologist Lev Vygotsky (1978) gave us two powerful tools that can be used to understand and further the integration of new students and their families into reforming schools: the Zone of Proximal Development (ZPD), which Vygotsky defines as the level of learning that a child can reasonably reach with the help of someone more skilled; and scaffolding, which is the act of creating small steps designed to bring the learner to the next level. The skilled teacher knows where her students are developmentally, what ZPD means in their case, and how to construct the appropriate scaffolds to bridge this gap. In social studies, for instance, upper elementary school students may be ready to understand empathizing with other children in countries far away where hunger is a serious problem. That readiness to empathize is their ZPD. Their teacher needs to find useful lessons and experiences that will help them move from simply knowing that hunger exists to really feeling for the plight of children around the

world. Those lessons are scaffolds built carefully for each child.

In integrating the new student into the reforming school, we need to add one element to our equation. The ZPD and the scaffolds go in both directions. Consider the four ways that innovating schools integrate new students described earlier in this chapter. In a traditional school, the new student's ZPD might be understanding the norms and expectations of the new school and finding a way to fit into that mold.

As we have seen, at reforming schools, the goal is much richer (see Figure 8.3): These schools strive for a ZPD in which the school can learn from the new student and change accordingly, as well as have the new student find a comfortable home in the new school. If mutual bridging is the goal, the structures described above are the scaffolds. For example, the more flexible curriculum-instruction-assessment patterns are not less demanding than more rigid patterns found in other schools. One major difference, however, is that they allow students of many different learning backgrounds to find a place, and they give the school a new ability to transform itself to connect with students. By communicating constantly with students to identify how they might learn best, and trying out new approaches to meet individual needs, the innovating school is learning from students. The students, often joined by family members, are constructing scaffolds for the school professionals and are helping them move to the next stage of development. In this way, the schools are following an important pattern described by Vygotsky and they are applying that pattern to their own organizational development.

Schools Scaffolding Students

Because scaffolding needs to go both ways, we need to consider how the school community can help new students and their families find a productive home, and how the school can learn to change through the influence of new members. The first half of the problem may be more familiar to administrators and teachers, as they often share school handbooks, send home letters with instructions for school procedures, and conduct opening-of-school assemblies to introduce new students. The common practice of using

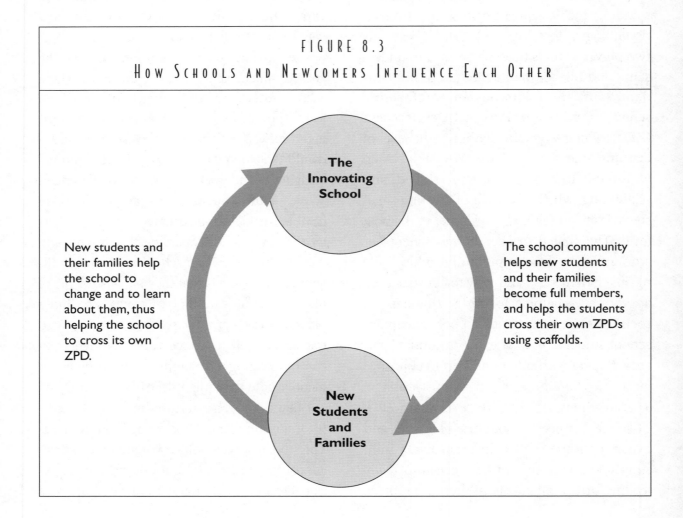

FIGURE 8.3
HOW SCHOOLS AND NEWCOMERS INFLUENCE EACH OTHER

The Innovating School

New students and their families help the school to change and to learn about them, thus helping the school to cross its own ZPD.

The school community helps new students and their families become full members, and helps the students cross their own ZPDs using scaffolds.

New Students and Families

homerooms or advisories is another, more interactive way to help students adjust, as are guidance services. Less common is the use of veteran student-new student pairings to help in the transition, although this is not a completely novel idea. Except for pairing, most of these practices lack the element of individual attention and are not likely to create a deep appreciation of the new school. New students certainly need to understand procedures, especially in the early stages of adjustment. Yet their longer lasting need is to learn about the deeper qualities of the school, including its norms and its possibilities.

I would strongly suggest that new students be paired with mentors of some sort. The most able students will actually cultivate mentoring relationships where none currently exist. As we saw in Challenge 1, mentoring relationships can be intense. A mentor with too many protégés probably finds it impossible to work effectively with them all. Therefore, schools might find it advisable to pair newcomers with individuals other than fellow students. Each school has faculty it can call on, of course, but many other adults can be found who could serve equally well with some training: retired faculty, for instance, or members of civic organizations, supportive businesses, or nonprofits. Prospective mentors should develop a strong familiarity with the school before establishing long-term relationships with a small group of students.

Students Scaffolding Schools

Schools that really want to learn from newcomers need to know who the new students are at any given moment, and what ideas, needs, goals, and special talents they bring. Schools could acquire such data through paper questionnaires, but why not bring the process to life by holding in-depth interviews with new students and their families? Students in social studies classes could be trained to conduct interviews, record them, and build a rich, continually renewed database of information (see Figure 8.4 for some possible interview questions). In addition, schools could initiate and compile dialogues among new students.

Once the information is gathered, schools need a way to analyze it and put it to use. Shared governance seems quite appropriate for this purpose. Teachers and administrators could create a subcommittee to sift through interview and dialogue data for important trends. This information could be refined and sent back to the new students and their families in the form of a questionnaire, to ensure that they are the most important issues for the school. The data-analysis process can even be built into strategic planning, thus formalizing the process of change, and should be conducted several times a year, every year. In doing so, the school will build a powerful longitudinal record of its students, and send an equally powerful message of sincere concern for students.

FIGURE 8.4

POSSIBLE INTERVIEW QUESTIONS FOR NEW STUDENTS

---

1. Describe something that you really enjoyed learning.

2. When you are excited about something you are learning, are you usually alone, with friends, or with a large class?

3. Do you like to learn by doing, by watching, or by listening?

4. What was a bad school experience that you would like to avoid repeating?

5. Think of a teacher that you liked a lot. How did she help you learn?

Supporting Advanced Teacher-Learners

9

ADVANCED TEACHER-LEARNERS ARE THOSE WHO HAVE SPENT YEARS IN AN innovating school, perhaps from its inception, and typically have at least seven years of teaching experience. These educators consistently set and meet personal and community learning goals; they are career leaders who have elected to remain in the classroom and serve as stellar models for their colleagues, both in the innovating school and beyond.

After studying the work of advanced teacher-learners in several schools that have sustained innovation for over a decade, I found that these schools had five integrated themes in common:

1. A powerful reform environment
2. A community of shared values
3. A principal who helps promote creativity
4. A faculty-created curriculum
5. A commitment to deep development

Each of these elements is related to the others, and all are related to aspects of the school that we have already discussed in this book, such as teacher leadership and shared governance.

A Powerful Reform Environment

Although it may seem obvious from the stories told so far, the environment of reforming schools is itself a strong stimulant to the continued performance and development of veteran teachers. At one of the suburban high schools I visited, teacher teams helped build a freshman/sophomore house, expand project-based learning, refine team teaching, design an advanced placement course in U.S. history, and further the work of their shared governance process. Because these projects were rooted in the school's agenda building process, they were tied to the concerns and priorities of the faculty.

Administrators at reforming schools don't have to plead for participation, since, in the words of one longtime teacher, "You cannot be a teacher here and not collaborate." Working on reforms and seeing the direct results of their work helps reward teachers and promote their continued engagement. Take the team that created the freshman/sophomore house, for instance. In this case, a group of interested teachers met each Tuesday for a year, and sometimes worked for whole days. Knowing that their colleagues and students were counting on them, the teachers needed to be focused and pragmatic. In the words of one participant, the process was "intense"—yet also highly rewarding. It struck me as the kind of intense demand that

is often placed upon honored professionals in such fields as medicine or the law.

Knowing that no school can lay claim to perfection, innovating educators act as though continued growth is natural and attractive. As one elementary school teacher put it, "We are always striving but never arriving." If you think you have arrived, you have only stopped growing. One guidance counselor at an urban high school thought about it this way:

> This school's been reformed over and over again. I think that this has allowed people to remain interested. It's such a vital environment and change is encouraged.... If you want to do different things, if you want to get into different areas, if you want to try administration, if you want to try counseling, there are just so many opportunities ... and I think that when you have an innovative staff it rubs off. So, excited innovative people create other people who are likeminded.

The stimulating atmosphere at reforming schools should be predictable and not overcharged. One elementary school teacher reflected that it was the expectation of reasonable change built into a stable school that kept her interest alive. Elements of this changing environment included the challenges of teaching new children every year, competing with previous successes inside the school and beyond, and working with colleagues and their highly respected principal to refine the school's approach to education.

A Community of Shared Values

In a community of shared values, educators work on individually rewarding projects and establish an expanded sense of common enterprise. These communities are hardly perfect, needing continuous nurturing and adjustment, but they are alive with the communication of plans, advice for those who are struggling, and celebrations of successes. Shared governance is important, of course, but community is created in other ways as well. At one school I researched, interdisciplinary teams met to design curriculum innovations and refine instructional approaches. Some schools also have more informal structures for bringing teachers together: At Burruss Elementary School, for instance, educators knew when any of their colleagues were expecting babies and made sure to pay them visits in the hospital. Although such familial relationships may also exist in noninnovating schools, the difference is that reforming teachers are connected by a shared dedication to continued reform.

Sometimes, an embracing community can even alter a teacher's career. One high school teacher told me about the time personal and developmental difficulties nearly drove him from the profession. It was his colleagues who made the difference. At this teacher's school, community and a sense of history were literally mapped on a huge paper timeline. Everyone was free to contribute to the timeline by noting something that they had done over the course of the school's life. One teacher wrote about participating in a math and science institute, another about helping to create a new course, and still others about their family lives during the course of the school's progress from conception to action. The timeline was brought to the annual retreat and stood as a living example of likeminded people contributing to a vibrant and effective educational experiment. It helped the teacher in question to see the larger picture of his work and how connected he was to the lives of valued colleagues and students, thus helping to end his sense of isolation.

A Principal Who Helps Promote Creativity

The principals at the schools I studied were, in partnership with the faculty and staff, keepers of their schools' visions. At times, they stated that they needed to be just a little ahead of the rest of the school, to see just over the next curve. They were not manipulating the faculty by trying to stay ahead, but rather doing their work effectively. In Challenge 4, we will see just how crucial this kind of leadership can be in sustaining the reform agenda.

Another way these principals helped keep veteran teacher-learners going was by opening the road to their new ideas. At an urban high school, one teacher told me that the first remark his principal made after hearing a new idea was, "What do you want? How can I help you get there?" At that same school, a lead teacher explained her principal's way of facilitating new ideas as follows: "He gives teachers freedom to do what they think is good for students, and he trusts them to do it. . . . You have an idea, and you go talk to him. He doesn't shoot you down . . . he says, 'OK, try it and then let's evaluate it.'"

Two things are important to note from this recollection. First, the principal was open to new ideas and willing to try many of them out. This means that teachers with a fresh approach may feel more likely to bring it up without the fear of ridicule. Naturally, this openness takes a good deal of confidence on the part of the principal. The second thing to note from the recollection is the systematic process for introducing new ideas. Reforming principals and teachers tend to craft clear procedures for starting new directions and expanding the agenda. At the schools I studied, new ideas normally had trial periods during which effects were measured carefully and reviewed by collegial groups of teachers. Such processes free the principal to support new ideas.

Innovating principals are neither laissez-faire nor guardians at the gates. Rather, their role is to blend the vision of the school with a measured system for allowing new ideas to emerge.

A Faculty-Created Curriculum

Advanced teacher-learners at reforming schools enjoy developing creative approaches to curriculum. They see the curriculum as their own responsibility, rather than as work inherited from the district or state. Although the curriculum plans of reforming schools are certainly influenced by external expectations, the development of these plans is guided by the teachers' and administrators' own wishes for their students.

At one high school I studied, teachers planned an interim session activity for a small group of students. One year, the group expanded the traditional curriculum through hiking and camping. The teachers approached the camping trip the same way they did classroom teaching: They planned carefully, used feedback to inform their actions, listened carefully to students, and were dedicated to constant revision. In other words, they were constructing a professional development activity that also led to expanded learning for students and was linked to the school's learning objectives and reform efforts.

One teacher told me that curriculum control was central to staying charged up after years of teaching: "We're pretty much in control of what we do in our classrooms. No one gives us a curriculum from on high and says these are the kinds of things that you are going to do in your classrooms over the course of the next year. If we're bored, we're bored by choice, not by fiat."

A Commitment to Deep Development

Whether thinking about the reforming environment, appreciating the benefits of a focused community, or feeling a sense of ownership for the curriculum, reforming teachers are engaged in deep development. One of the reforming principals I met attributed the deep development at his school to its governing structure:

> The governing structure of this school parallels the relationships and special strategies that we hope teachers will use in classrooms. [Both involve] organizing people into small collaborative groups for the purposes of exploring the content at hand and supporting one another's learning. The faculty ... makes the important decisions about what kids need to learn and how best they can learn it, how to assess that learning, and how to apply resources. ... So it is the governing structure of the school that parallels and supports the instructional model in the classroom.

At some of the schools I researched, deep development was manifested in the lives of teachers through retreats during which annual goals were set. At weekly team meetings, the teachers would focus on these goals to make them come alive. Teachers often came to school early and left late and even spent extra days in school because they wanted to work hard on the innovations that they helped to put in place. Peer coaching and reflecting on new instructional techniques also kept these teachers focused on their own growth.

At Oceana High School, the annual retreats set themes that united all growth for the coming year. One year, the retreat focused on the struggling student. The whole school community asked serious questions: What do we know about struggling students at our school? How might our own teaching styles and teacher-student relationships bear on this problem? Data showed that 10th graders at the school were in the worst shape; 9th graders, who had many supports in place, seemed to do better in school. This gave the group, which was composed of all the teachers and administrators in the school, an idea: If the freshman house seemed to help 9th graders, why not expand it to include sophomores? The teachers soon got to work designing and helping to implement this new stage of the school's reform.

The previous year, the same annual planning process had led to the development of senior portfolios and exhibitions. Through deep development, the teachers had learned from students that due dates were a pivotal issue. Although administrators might have made this kind of decision alone in a more traditional school, innovating teachers like to be involved. Unfortunately, the due dates for the portfolios conflicted with fall SAT tests and college application deadlines. Students and families soon protested, and the calendar was changed. Teachers stayed involved until the details were ironed out, the innovative senior portfolios completed, and a workable schedule was in place. Working a problem to completion is a hallmark of reforming teachers' professionalism.

In another case, mentoring served as a deep development activity. Veteran teachers studied the kinds of teaching they wanted to pass along to novice teachers, along with the most effective ways to do so. They traveled for professional training in the new methods. This is a wonderful example of teachers moving away from merely being accountable to external authority, and toward greater personal responsibility for schoolwide instruction. Though I certainly heard stories specific to teachers' classrooms, more often I heard about instruction in a much broader sense, with teachers speaking about being members of a world community of educators.

Action Strategy: Erikson's Psychosocial Crises

The faculty of any school is commonly a mix of different talents, ages, and approaches to life. In many preservice teacher education programs, students learn to better understand some of these variables through the study of developmental theory, which teaches us that certain kinds of learning may be easier or more difficult at different developmental stages. The work of Jean Piaget is perhaps what first comes to mind when we talk about developmental theory. But the work of Erik Erikson also deserves our attention. According to Erikson (1980), we go through eight psychosocial crises in our lives. He refers to these stages as "crises" because during each one, we are faced with diametrically opposed choices about our future.

The first crisis, which Erikson calls Trust vs. Mistrust, occurs during the first few months after birth, when babies either learn to interact comfortably with the powerful adults in their lives or withdraw into themselves. During the early school years, children face the third crisis, Industry vs. Inferiority, when children either learn to work effectively in school and get rewarded for it, or sink into feelings of inferiority and failure. This stage lasts through elementary school.

In middle and high school, students are at the Identity vs. Role Defusion stage. Here, adolescents work hard to learn who they are as human beings. Those who have spent time with teenagers or who remember their own youth will be familiar with the seemingly endless efforts to wear just the right clothes or behave in the most sophisticated way. At the same time, these teens are anxious to find their own place in the world. What many of us too quickly dismiss as poor manners, immaturity, or self-absorption are more accurately seen as energetic reactions to impending independence.

Important as Erikson's work is for us as we think about the students we face in our classrooms, it is just as powerful a lens through which to think about teachers. Understanding the psychosocial stages is remarkably useful for helping us understand the needs of advanced teacher-learners. Teachers in their late 20s and early 30s are facing the crisis of Intimacy vs. Isolation. At this stage, we are looking for life partners and long-term friendships. We also need to find communities where we are accepted. It is easy to see how the innovating school can fill some of those needs by providing a strong supporting community, authentic collegial relationships, and a cause worth identifying with as central to our lives. I believe that it is because innovating schools do this that they receive so much energy and dedication in return. By recognizing these personal developmental needs of younger veteran faculty, schools can continue to build upon their agenda while also

helping key people in their midst solve crucial issues and meet deep-seated needs.

Middle-aged teachers are facing Erikson's seventh psychosocial crisis: Generativity vs. Self-Absorption. At this stage, people need to find ways to pass their knowledge and growing wisdom along to younger adults. If this is not done effectively, they face the possibility of growing ever inward to the point of shutting off outside responsibilities and connections. When older veterans mentor novice teachers, or help guide curriculum even though they might never see the fruits of those efforts, they are being generative. I remember one school where new teachers were brought directly into teams of veteran teachers, many of whom had 25 years of experience. Not wanting to leave the new teachers to sink or swim, the veterans agreed to each pair up with a novice. I wish you could have seen the faces of those experienced teachers as they shared with and guided the new teachers. They clearly knew that they were imparting their own approaches to life and to the profession to a new generation. Just as compelling were the perspectives of the young teachers, who were forming strongly rooted teaching identities.

One way to look at the wonderful contributions made by veteran teachers is to think of them as working out crucial issues in their own lives and meeting some of their own highest priorities. Giving them authentic and meaningful opportunities to do so allows us all to move with the currents of our lives and use the power of our human emotions. By understanding that older veterans need to find ways to pass along their gifts, we can see the issue of teacher burnout in a new light: Maybe the problem is not with the teachers, but with a system that has caused them to turn inward from frustration.

Erikson's work helps us to understand the life cycle in new ways that are particularly relevant to reforming schools. We are all private people dealing with public responsibilities as best we can; as planners, being sensitive to this fact can help us blend our natural drives with the patterns of reform.

Applying Erikson's Psychosocial Crisis Model in Your Setting

The following exercise is designed to help teachers, staff members, and administrators in reforming schools to connect Erikson's psychosocial crises to their own lives, both individually and as a group.

Step 1. Divide all teachers, staff, and administrators into mixed groups of four. Have each person reflect upon the questions and complete the grid in Figure 9.1, which are meant to provoke thoughts on the Intimacy vs. Isolation and Generativity vs. Self-Absorption crises.

Step 2. Because each crisis is a struggle between two alternatives, one positive and one negative, it is essential that we find out what in the school may be keeping us from finding intimacy and generativity and pushing us toward isolation and self-absorption. To do this, have each person in the group reflect upon the questions and complete the grid in Figure 9.2.

Step 3. After your group has combined its responses on the two grids, combine the responses for all of the groups to see where commonalities exist. This may be efficiently done by hanging all of the grids on the walls of a room and asking participants to walk past them, noting important similarities and differences.

Step 4. With the help of a whole group facilitator, identify the key forces that encourage and discourage intimacy and generativity.

Now your school's community will have some detailed ideas about both the positive and negative forces surrounding Erickson's developmental stages. Qualities that may go unnoticed by the groups—such as personality, personal history, gender, race, national origin, religious beliefs, and sexual orientation—can also greatly influence our approaches to life, but this exercise, and an understanding of Erickson's stages, can provide some powerful keys to sustaining your school's long-term teachers.

FIGURE 9.1
QUESTION AND ANSWER GRID #1

Question	Response	Response	Response	Response	Combined Response
1. What in my life helps me to feel that I belong to something larger than myself?					
2. What in my work helps me to feel that I belong to something larger than myself?					
3. How is my work connected to others in a satisfying way?					
4. How am I helping to pass on wisdom that I have gained from my professional life?					

FIGURE 9.2
QUESTION AND ANSWER GRID #2

Question	Response	Response	Response	Response	Combined Response
1. What in my school life keeps me from working with others on common projects?					
2. When do I feel most alone in my work life when I would rather not be alone?					
3. What blocks me from passing on my knowledge to newer colleagues?					
4. What keeps me focused on my own situation so that I do not have the time to think about the school in the years after I leave?					

Conclusion to Challenge 3

BECAUSE SCHOOL CULTURES ARE FLUID AND DYNAMIC, ATTEMPTING TO keep things just as they are and closing your school off to new ideas is a poor strategy. Schools need to act to assure the successful integration of new teachers, students, and families; those that have sustained innovation for a decade or more tend to have done so, and tend to be careful in the prehiring process as well. Mentoring and other intensive professional development approaches can provide teachers with successful early experiences and limit the chances for failure. New hires, as well as new students and families, should be seen as great resources for schools that are not to be wasted.

At the heart of a school's practice is the dynamic curriculum-instruction-assessment triangle, which represents a commitment to reach out to new students and learn from them that is built into the very DNA of the school. Yet what good would the triangle be if veteran teachers, many of whom helped implement reforms in the first place, are ignored? Instead of taking these teachers for granted, the reforming schools I studied treated them as advanced teacher-learners by giving them resources and opportunities to continue their practice and lead the way for new teachers.

Challenge 4

Governing a large country is like frying a small fish: You spoil it with too much poking.

—Lao-Tse

Steering an Honorable Course Through External Upheavals

FIGURE C-4
TURBULENCE GAUGE FOR CHALLENGE 4

Degree of Turbulence	General Definition	Relevant Scenario
Light	Associated with ongoing issues Little or no disruption to the normal work environment Subtle signs of stress	Strong alliances with the district support continued reform efforts. State and federal programs encourage current efforts and require only a straightforward continuation of past work.
Moderate	Widespread awareness of the issue and its specific origins	The central office is being pressured to move away from earlier support of the school's reform. Serious curriculum mapping is conducted to try to keep the school's program aligned to state and federal mandates. A great deal of continuing work will be required, sapping resources and energy.
Severe	Possibility of large-scale community demonstrations A sense of crisis	A chief ally in the central office may have been replaced with an unsympathetic character. State and federal legislation seems poised to cause serious damage to some key elements of the school's reform.
Extreme	Structural damage to the school's reform Collapse of the reform seems likely	Changes in the central office mean the district is now hostile to school reform efforts. State and federal requirements threaten almost all previous work. The school may have been placed on a list of underperforming sites.

Challenge 4

Schools that work hard to improve learning for students often have a close-knit community of likeminded professionals, and a learning program that is frequently the result of intensive work from nearly everyone in the building over many years. These schools are also likely to have earned the trust of community members and families, of whom many will have sent children to the school, which may become part of their extended family.

Although it is tempting to see these schools as ships on their own difficult but rewarding adventures, this is a fantasy. Public schools exist inside of districts, which are in turn responsible to states. Even independent schools must respond to the demands of the larger world, since they are doomed if people stop paying tuition. It is therefore vital for reforming leaders at all levels to understand the world beyond their doors. Changes in district leadership will likely have serious consequences. Similarly, changes in state law, such as the current accountability movement and high stakes testing, are almost certain to have a powerful effect on the learning programs that define innovating schools. Finally, with the introduction of new federal legislation such as No Child Left Behind, national pressure is being aimed at all schools that accept federal funding.

No school that hopes to sustain its innovations for long can afford to ignore these forces, and this section will help you to consider ways that you might respond effectively to them. I will also introduce you to the story of one school that had to recast its vision altogether without selling out its core mission.

Consult the Turbulence Gauge for Challenge 4 (Figure C-4) to determine whether this section is relevant to your current situation.

10

Dealing Effectively With District Leadership

ALTHOUGH THE ACCOUNTS OF INNOVATIVE SCHOOLS IN THIS BOOK SO FAR have centered on life at the school level, it is obvious that these institutions do not live in a vacuum. Except for the Red Cedar School, which is independent, all the reforming schools I visited are public and thus must relate somehow to larger organizational demands. Often, it was the district itself that started or supported the kind of serious change that initiated reforms in the first place: At Oceana High School, for example, it was the superintendent who gave Lois Jones and her colleagues the charge of reinventing their school. Funding and other crucial management processes originate in the district, and so does oversight. In addition to supervising building-level activities, central office administrators normally are the first to meet with school board members, who are responsible for establishing district policy. Although our system of public education leaves this enterprise to the state, the district and the board have a great deal of influence, so the relationship that the innovating school establishes with the central office is crucial.

A Tale of Three Districts

You are about to read three examples of districts and their relationships with the reforming schools within them. The first case shows a supportive district that sees no barrier between the life of its reforming schools and its own future. In the second case, we will consider a district that needs to unite to support reform in the face of public opposition. The third case shows how a change in central office personnel contributed to the demise of reform at one school.

Example #1: District Support of Reform in Paragould, Arkansas

In *Staying Centered,* I discussed the reforming work of the schools in the city of Paragould, Arkansas. Not only did I find a great deal of innovation going on at all levels in this district, from infants to high school students, but I discovered that this work was part of a larger pattern: The district itself meant to promote innovation at its schools, and considered this kind of work essential for its students. The superintendent, school board, administrators, and teachers were all seen as part of a development team. Naturally, not all of the efforts were perfect, and some did not last; the point is that the district encouraged the schools to experiment.

The central office and the school board also saw it as their responsibility to make sure that the reforms were not over stimulating. This led to a Future Search process, in which a group of teachers, students, administrators, and board members worked together to figure out what they valued, what they wanted to keep, and what they could trim. The district also established a process for new ideas

that took reforms from the drawing board through to the evaluation stage. Many new programs started, and got a fair chance to prove themselves. The district review process for innovating programs typically leads to some programs being shut down while others are modified and reviewed again, but the transparency at Paragould encouraged change within agreed-upon guidelines. The district took its responsibility to lead change seriously and helped each school to identify areas for development. This led to variety and greater freedom to make decisions at the school level, yet did not result in chaos because the district took coordination and policymaking seriously.

I found the same kind of district support evident in the case of Oceana High School, where the district helped a new principal to succeed through a highly interactive mentoring program. This program received financial support from the district and was connected to the superintendent's office. The mentor and her protégé sent agendas of their meetings to the superintendent's office, and met with him at least once a year to discuss the progress and future of the mentor-protégé relationship. Eventually, the district elected to support the program for three years.

In both cases, the central office showed an understanding of its role in helping to sustain reform at the building level; in Paragould, the district saw the big picture and understood that the various elements of reform needed to be connected to form a larger coherent vision. Although teacher-student relationships are obviously essential, districts must address all of their students' educational relationships, from the earliest years until graduation. Even in an era of high mobility, districts must design their work to include at least K–12 curriculum-instruction-assessment continuity. Elementary school reforms need to be sustained through middle and high school to ensure that students don't feel intellectually disconnected by a disjointed learning program.

Example #2: The Struggle to Sustain Reform in Verona, Wisconsin

In Verona, Wisconsin, I found an equally high degree of district support for reform, but with a twist: Whereas most in Paragould seemed satisfied with the district's general direction, the district in Verona was emerging from a serious division when I visited. Part of the community supported recent district reforms, while others complained that the schools were moving away from the basics.

If they spend too much time considering the possibility of a public backlash, central office leaders may hesitate to try new ideas. In the case of Verona, the central office took a different stance. Listening carefully to thoughtful community members, the district opened the lines of communication and held large forums facilitated by a trusted community leader with group dynamic skills. These meetings were also televised on cable so that anyone in the area could see their progress. Because the group was inclusive, many different points of view were heard.

The patient work of district leaders and board members brought the schools of Verona back from controversy to a place of new development. In fact, the district's assumption of responsibility led to such innovations as the establishment of Wisconsin's first charter schools. The experience was described as painful by many—and as a learning experience by almost everyone: People from schools all over town learned something about their organizations, their community, and even themselves as a result. Because the issues over reform were so heated, with many people on either side, it was not possible for leaders to simply walk away from the conflict. They needed to own the process and the results it yielded.

Example #3: Foundering Reforms in Crafton Elementary School

Located in a metropolitan area, Crafton Elementary School had a successful reform program that included an enriched curriculum, strong technology support in lesson planning, professional development, continuous contact with families, and a novel community outreach program. The superintendent was a key supporter of the school, and even

Reform Efforts at the District Level	
Building-Level Support	Whole District Design

1. Districts can initiate or support specific reform programs at individual schools.

2. District officials can see the whole district as the location for reform and coordinate efforts for all the schools in a preK–12 continuum.

wanted to spread its program to other schools in the district.

Then the superintendent left, and a new one was hired. The new leader had heard of the Crafton program, but she did not strongly support it, let alone want to spread it to other schools. Although there were other serious

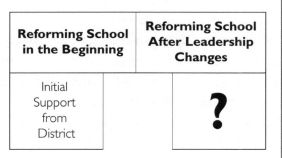

Reforming School in the Beginning	Reforming School After Leadership Changes
Initial Support from District	**?**

Here, we see that reform was supported by the district when it was begun. However, with a change in central office leadership, reform was no longer a top concern and support dried up, leaving the future of innovation in doubt.

challenges leading to the demise of program, the lack of a strong district-level ally was clearly a problem, and almost impossible to overcome. Where the school had once been an outstanding example for others to learn from, it was now an island and vulnerable to district and state pressures to follow different approaches.

A Closer Look at District Leadership Changes

The challenge for districts that support successful reform is straightforward: School and district leaders need to stay in close contact, monitor one another's work, and conduct periodic reviews of the reform program to sustain confidence at all levels. As an added challenge, districts may need to conceptualize reform at the school system level so that innovative schools aren't isolated from others. These steps are essential for reforming schools to continue their enviable relationship with district leaders and to ensure their place within the larger organization.

At many schools that have achieved success, the challenges are much more serious. Like Crafton, these schools may see the district as uninterested at best, and working counter to the reform agenda at worst. It is vital for these schools to consider strategic options.

The following scenarios illustrate some common difficulties that schools have with central administration.

Scenario #1: New External Pressures on the District Threaten Support for Reforms

When things were calm and there was sufficient time, the district seemed to smile upon the reforming school—indeed, the impetus for change even came from the district itself. Now, however, things have changed: The economy has gone sour, and parents and business leaders are starting to ask the school to cut the budget of "frills," which may include professional development money. Support for new school-based initiatives has all but evaporated, and a tax revolt looms. As we will see in the next chapter, the accountability movement itself may have pushed a once-sympathetic district administrator away from the reforming school.

It is essential for school-based and district leaders to understand that external factors may cause such pressure that they can no longer stand behind even productive experiments. This raises the question of initial expectations: Was the reforming school initially seen by the central office as the vanguard of district change? If so, was that made part of the initial agreement between the district and the school's leadership, faculty, and staff? If there was an agreement to spread the reform ideas to other schools, was there a coherent plan or only an impressionistic vision? Does the reform lend itself to replication or is it unique to a given population? One high school I researched developed a curriculum and a culture that was very academic and excluded varsity sports. Clearly, this had support from students and parents. However, if the district were to decide upon this direction for all of its schools, it would mean, in effect, a ban on such sports—a prospect not likely to win universal praise in many communities. Though we are no longer looking at schools in the first phases of development, it is still possible to revisit formal and informal initial agreements to make sure that a shared understanding of expectations exists.

Scenario #2: New Leadership and the Lack of Ownership of Reform

In one district, a new superintendent pursued a basal reading program at a reforming school that several of the teachers felt was at odds with their long-standing efforts at constructivist learning. While this new direction seemed attached to a desire to increase standardized test scores, the issue also seemed related to the fact that this district leader was not in on reform from the start. Did this new leader understand the meaning of reform in this successful school? Did he appreciate the specifics that led to the adoption of a reading program that included a good deal of nonbasal literature? Or was there a need to look at the system as a whole, rather than at the schools individually, because of external pressures? This is another example of state accountability programs playing out at the local level. In this case, however, there is no track record of support from the administrator. We cannot be sure what he believes in, how much change he is looking for, or what his tolerance is for creative and successful alternatives to the district norm.

Because of the questions above, leaders of building-based innovations are likely to feel uncomfortable with a new district leader who does not have a professional affiliation with their type of reform program. This raises important questions surrounding the selection of new central office leadership (see Figure 10.1):

What was the new leader's mandate? Was she asked by the board to sustain diversity in the schools, or was there pressure for a uniform approach?

What role, if any, did the faculty, staff, and administration of the reforming school have in the selection of the new district leadership? Whether or not these particular school professionals were central to the selection process will tell a great deal about the relative value that the board places on their work.

How is the innovating school viewed by the district? Is it an interesting outlier? Is it an important laboratory for experimentation? Is it in the vanguard of where the district hopes to go? In architectural terms, is the reforming school window dressing, or is it the keystone of the district's edifice of education? If there is no shared answer to this question, that tells us something of the marginal status of the reforming school in the district's worldview.

As leaders in the innovating school consider likely answers to these questions, they can estimate the degree to which they can expect district support.

Action Strategy: Understanding Political Power

Although it is a mistake to overestimate the role of politics in school affairs, it is probably naïve to ignore this aspect of organizational life. In his book *Images of Organization* (1997), Gareth Morgan demonstrates the powerful use of metaphors in helping us to understand how organizations operate over time. For instance, when organizations become bureaucratic, we may think of them as machines; when we try to evolve in response to changes in our environment, we may be said to operate like organisms; and when we strive to become learning organizations, we are most like the brain. In all, Morgan identifies eight metaphors, describing their usefulness for decoding the underlying facts of life in our institutions.

Morgan also helps us to see the strengths and limits of any one metaphor. In his words, metaphors both illuminate *and* obscure reality. I will use the concept of the political

FIGURE 10.1
FORCES THAT AFFECT THE NEW LEADER'S VIEW OF THE REFORMING SCHOOL

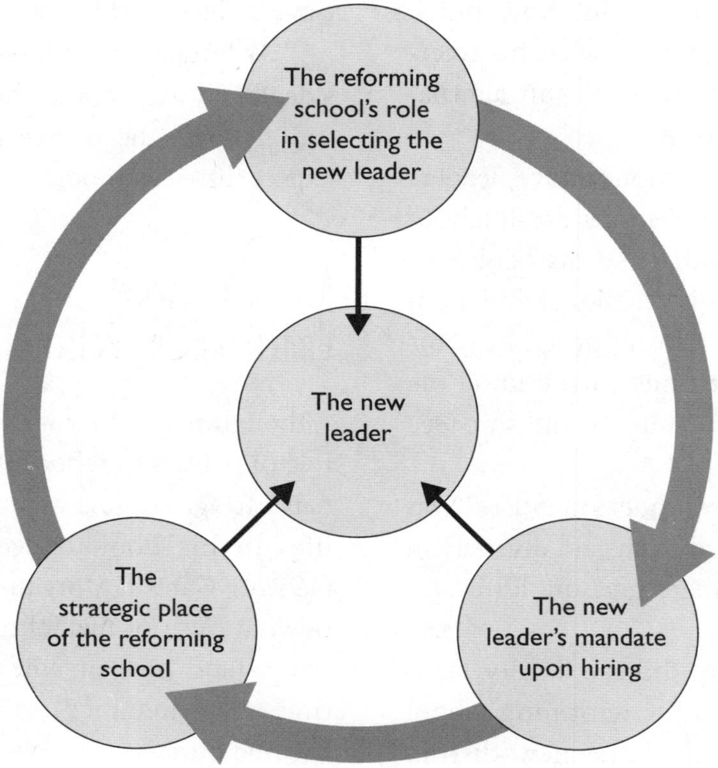

The degree to which a school helps select a new superintendent may affect not only its strategic place in the district's future plans, but the superintendent's mandate, which will itself also affect the school's strategic place in the district.

metaphor here as a way of thinking through the power relationships that exist in a district—to help us see where the central office has power, where the individual school does, and where their power is shared. Still, we should remember Morgan's caveat: Though this metaphor will illuminate, it will also obscure reality if used to the exclusion of other lenses. Political realities are powerful, but they are not the only realities.

In his book, Morgan describes the following 14 sources of power, which I have applied to school or district settings:

1. Formal Authority. The formal hierarchy of the district and the schools that make it up. We invest leaders with authority, some of which is legally derived, some of which is there by tradition and custom.

2. Control of Scarce Resources. These include money, materials, technology, and personnel. Examples include school or district budgets, hiring, class size, classrooms, and materials needed to operate the schools.

3. Use of Organizational Structures, Rules, and Regulations. Who sets the formal rules within a district or school? What does their structure mean? Who is stronger by virtue of these agreements? Who is weaker?

4. Control of Decision Processes. Controlling the processes means controlling the outcome. What rules guide board decisions? How is the reforming school to be evaluated? Who makes that decision?

5. Control of Knowledge and Information. Where information is power, this is vital. What counts as results in the school? Does this impact the reforming school differently than other schools in the district?

6. Control of Boundaries. Those who control departments, schools, and access to the school board and organizations such as universities.

7. Ability to Cope with Uncertainty. Changes in state law can cause a great deal of uncertainty. Changes in local budgets can do likewise. The district has a great deal of power here but the reforming school can also influence things.

8. Control of Technology. On the surface, this means computers, networking, and software. But there is also a technology of learning that has changed over time. The reforming school may be a leader in this area, but it might be controlled by district regulations, such as policies on access to Web pages.

9. Interpersonal Alliances, Networks, and Control of the Informal Organization. Here the reforming school may have as many relationships beyond the district as the central office. These may or may not be aligned, with cooperation, depending on history and local custom.

10. Control of Counterorganizations. Teacher, administrator, and staff unions have an effect on both the local and national levels. Both the National Education Association (NEA) and the American Federation of

Teachers (AFT) have longstanding positions on reform.

11. Symbolism and the Management of Meaning. As Morgan notes, "The democratic leader's influence is far more subtle and symbolic. He or she spends time listening, summarizing, integrating, and guiding what is being said, making key interventions and summoning images, ideas, and values that help those involved to make sense of the situation with which they are dealing" (1997, p. 176). Example: shared governance models.

12. Gender and the Management of Gender Relations. This is crucial for all organizations, but is a particularly pointed issue in schools. Traditionally, women have been found in the classroom but not in administrative positions at the district level. While there is movement away from this unequal pattern, there is still a paucity of women in leadership positions, especially in the central office. Women may have a strong influence upon reform efforts at the building level, but be at a disadvantage as they negotiate a more male culture at the district level.

13. Structural Factors that Define the Stage of Action. Whereas the district may have formal control over the school, this power may be counterbalanced by the community's strong support of the schools reforms.

14. The Power One Already Has. Everyone in the district has some kind of power, which can be strengthened or weakened by our reactions to events. We need to be aware of our power and able to find effective ways to build upon it.

Clearly, some sources of power apply more to the districts than to reforming schools. It would be a mistake, however, to assume that the reforming school has little power, or that there is little overlapping power. For instance, teachers and administrators at one school I researched carefully used their political power by joining other innovating high schools, thereby increasing their influence at the state level. This is not an argument for the creation of conflict between reforming schools and the district—just the opposite. Wise leadership teams at every level will consider this list of power sources and determine where they might exercise influence. The educators at the high school mentioned above had a keen sense of the power they already possessed, and how to maximize it throughout the city and region. These educators felt they were fighting for the best interests of their students against what they saw as an intrusive state plan. In this way, the reforming school and the district might bridge differences and come to a shared vision of the future. Neither one has all the elements of power, but neither is without its own impressive sources.

At its worst, this fact can lead to an impasse; thoughtfully navigated, it can lead to creative coordination of efforts.

Applying Morgan's Political Metaphor to Your Setting

Step 1: Gathering the Basics. The leadership team in your school and district should fill out the table in Figure 10.2 as specifically as possible, using recent real-life examples. When the table is complete, it should show that both the school and the central office have considerable power. Be sure to engage in dialogue throughout the exercise, so that a shared understanding can be established.

Step 2: Making Judgments. Now your school and district leadership team should evaluate the relative power that the school and district wield for each source. After filling out the chart in Figure 10.3, discuss how shared power can be expanded to help both the district and the school reach important goals.

Step 3: Changes Over Time. As a final step, review the current balance of power between the school and the district, then create another chart showing how things stood five years ago. This will help you to determine important power shifts. Reforming schools must understand and respond to the political realities surrounding them if they are to thrive under serious changes at the district office. The results of this analysis will give your school the tools with which to prove that in the pursuit of influence, it is not at baseline zero.

FIGURE 10.2
POWER CHART FOR YOUR SCHOOL AND DISTRICT

Source of Power	Example from the Central Office	Example from the School	Example Shared by the Central Office and the School
1. Formal Authority			
2. Control of Scarce Resources			
3. Use of Organizational Structures, Rules, and Regulations			
4. Control of Decision Processes			
5. Control of Knowledge and Information			
6. Control of Boundaries			
7. Ability to Cope with Uncertainty			
8. Control of Technology			
9. Interpersonal Alliances, Networks, and Control of the Informal Organization			
10. Control of Counterorganizations			
11. Symbolism and the Management of Meaning			
12. Gender and the Management of Gender Relations			
13. Structural Factors that Define the Stage of Action			
14. The Power One Already Has			

Note: Adapted from Morgan, G. (1997). *Images of organization* (p. 171). Thousand Oaks, CA: Sage Publications. Copyright © 1997 by Sage Publications. Reprinted by permission of Sage Publications.

FIGURE 10.3

VALUE JUDGMENT CHART FOR SCHOOL AND DISTRICT POWER

Source of Power	Example from the Central Office	Example from the School	Example Shared by the Central Office and the School
1. Formal Authority			
2. Control of Scarce Resources			
3. Use of Organizational Structures, Rules, and Regulations			
4. Control of Decision Processes			
5. Control of Knowledge and Information			
6. Control of Boundaries			
7. Ability to Cope with Uncertainty			
8. Control of Technology			
9. Interpersonal Alliances, Networks, and Control of the Informal Organization			
10. Control of Counter-organizations			
11. Symbolism and the Management of Meaning			
12. Gender and the Management of Gender Relations			
13. Structural Factors that Define the Stage of Action			
14. The Power One Already Has			

11

When the State and the Feds Come Marching In

AT THE TIME OF THIS WRITING, THE WORD "ACCOUNTABILITY" SEEMS TO BE everywhere. External pressures to prove that schools are effective are mounting. The signs of the accountability movement are easy to spot: For most, they come in the form of high-stakes testing that reflects upon students, teachers, schools, and districts. For students, low scores on such tests may mean they have to attend summer school or will not be able to graduate; for teachers, principals, and superintendents, they might threaten job security; and for districts they might mean a cut in funding— or in the most extreme case, state takeover of schools, as happened to all Philadelphia schools in 2001.

Early in 2002, the federal government added its weight to the accountability movement through the enactment of the No Child Left Behind law. This legislation seems destined to make a fundamental difference in the relationships between districts, states, and the federal government, and has already raised important questions about local control and decision-making. Clearly, the relevance of accountability to innovating schools, once free to invent on their own, is quite high.

Yet just because everyone uses the same word doesn't mean that we all have the same thing in mind. What different visions might we have in mind when we say the word "accountability"? In an earlier work, my colleagues and I reviewed the use of accountability in education in newspapers, magazines, and academic journals over the past 13 years (Gross, Shaw, & Shapiro, 2002). We wanted to know how different authors used the word, and to explain some of the pressures that these writers' visions might have upon schools. We wanted to know how people wrote about accountability and what changes they sought in schools to bring their version of accountability to life.

The results of our analysis were surprising. Rather than one clear definition for accountability with specific policy implications, we were able to create three clear categories, each stemming from a particular view of democracy: progressive, essentialist, and market driven (see Figure 11.1).

Progressives and Accountability

For progressives, democracy is tied to an active classroom, experiences beyond the schoolhouse that teach students about the outside world, and a great degree of local design in curriculum. Because progressive educators focus primarily on the needs of learners and on the creation of a community, they seek to support democracy through highly engaged classrooms, strong connections to families and communities, and ongoing authentic assessment. Accountability for progressives typically comes in the form of evidence from students, both individually and collectively, that they have achieved these goals (portfolios, for example). For progressives, accountability is largely the responsibility of the school, its families, and the surrounding community.

FIGURE 11.1
THREE TYPES OF ACCOUNTABILITY

Accountability for Progressives

This stems from attending to the needs of individual students as they are today and integrating them into the larger community through authentic experiences.

Accountability for Essentialists

This stems from all schools following one set of standards measured largely through scores on standardized tests.

Accountability for Market-Force Advocates

This stems from individuals making selections from a range of school choices, thereby creating a series of rewards and punishments for schools that attract or fail to attract students.

Essentialists and Accountability

Essentialists fear that our democracy is at risk due to increased economic competition, and that schools are poorly designed and lacking in rigor. They support state mandates for highly structured curriculum and regular standardized tests for all students as ways to foster educational equity among students. Essentialists normally measure accountability by analyzing standardized test results, and offer rewards and punishments as incentives and disincentives. For essentialists, accountability is largely the responsibility of the state and the federal government.

Market-Force Adherents and Accountability

In the market-driven view, education is a commodity and must fall into the same framework as other consumer choices in our society. This means that wise families need to have a range of options for their child, all held to certain standards of behavior. According to market-force advocates, democracy is best maintained when choice is available, because choice will lead to competition, leaving the best schools to surface as the most successful and the failing schools to shut down. Growth is therefore the reward for attracting new students, and the educational equivalent of bankruptcy is the consequence of poor performance. Accountability is achieved in this model when student customers vote with their feet and move in the direction of better schools. Families, making personal decisions within a fair market of choices, are seen as the primary responsible parties in this view of accountability.

As the above three examples make clear, there is no monolithic definition of accountability—what may seem like accountability to us might not satisfy others in our community or state. Further, these different definitions stem from philosophical differences rather than from objective evidence that can be proven one way or another.

In some ways, accountability is also a question of aesthetics: The movement and diversity of a progressive classroom may seem beautiful to its supporters, but appear chaotic to its critics; a teacher-centered essentialist classroom may appear well-ordered and logical to its creators but stifling to others; and the free choice offered by market-force advocates may look confusing, ugly, and out of control to both progressives and essentialists.

Policy leaders at all levels should also consider the implications of their actions down the chain of command. Figure 11.2 describes what I call the Lever Metaphor. The point of this metaphor is to remind all of us that we use power and that we need to be highly sensitive about its effect on others, whether they are near or far away from our daily lives.

FIGURE 11.2
THE LEVER METAPHOR

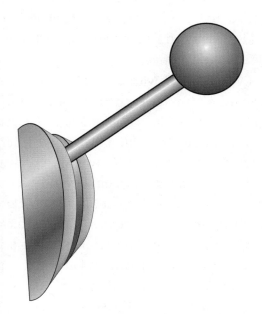

One way to get a sense of how responsible we really are is to think of decision making as pulling a lever:

- Students pull a lever when they determine how they will act at school,

- Teachers pull a lever each time they try to control classroom dynamics,

- Principals pull a lever whenever they make decisions that affect teachers,

- District administrators pull a lever when they allocate resources to schools,

- State legislators pull a lever whenever they pass mandates down to schools and districts, and

- The federal government pulls a lever when it enacts sweeping legislation such as the No Child Left Behind Act.

Though we are often sorely tempted to pull our levers, we need to remember all of those down the line whose lives will be changed when we do.

My colleague Joan Shapiro argues that the concept of "internal responsibility" offers an alternative to accountability that is more demanding and requires a higher ethical commitment. When we are accountable, we are extrinsically motivated to act a certain way: those in control are watching our work, and we need to make sure that they are impressed. When we are responsible, on the other hand, we are intrinsically motivated by our own vision and set of convictions. A sense of personal responsibility allows our humanity and professionalism to remain intact and respected, and is a value that all educators should pass along to their students.

Although we may speak of a pendulum swinging from progressive educational ideas to essentialist or traditional ones, it is also true that some almost always favor one or the other under any circumstances. It may seem that one side has dominated the discussion, but time nearly always shows that the other side will expand again when conditions change. We could use this as a powerful argument for diversity in our approaches. What many innovative schools must contend with, as we will see later in this chapter, are circumstances in which their space to be creative and demonstrate their philosophy is evaporating.

Curriculum and Accountability Challenges

Earlier in this book, I described the curriculum-instruction-assessment triangle and noted that whenever one of the triangle's three foci is subject to change, the other two foci are affected as well. In the current environment, the triangle as a whole seems under attack, with high-stakes assessments pressuring reforming schools to make difficult choices in instruction and curriculum—choices that can set their learning agendas off course.

Teachers and administrators at the schools I researched had strong reactions to their states' accountability measures. These educators' concerns often centered on the fact that the learning agenda at their schools was being set by someone far away. For instance, one teacher observed that his state's high-stakes tests don't "enable you to spend time to make connections . . . if you're working on the pilgrims or the Mayflower, how can you

possibly work on that without starting back on the Crusades? . . . You will not have enough time . . . the richness is lost." A teacher at another school said that the state required too many curricular changes too quickly, leaving no time to develop lessons and support materials.

Even schools with a highly structured curriculum can have their reform efforts derailed by state changes. Such was the case at one elementary school, where teachers wanted to use the Core Knowledge curriculum, but were thwarted when they discovered that new state tests did not align with Core Knowledge grade-level topics. These educators were left feeling helpless. Similarly, a science teacher at a high school famous for its successful innovations and student achievement lamented the school's adoption of a mandated Advanced Placement course that he believed would overemphasize facts at the expense of skills. This teacher also pointed out that the AP course might suggest to students that they can skip introductory courses in science once they enter college. As one of his department colleagues put it, the imposed AP courses "go very much against the ideas and philosophy of what the school was founded on."

As the Lever Metaphor in Figure 11.2 demonstrates, it is likely that changes made at higher levels of the educational system will have severe and sometimes unintended consequences at the ground level. It may be that no one at the state level really means to thwart programs like Core Knowledge, however, by pulling on the lever of action at their disposal, that seems to have been the result. In such cases, rich, demanding curriculum was placed at risk, quite possibly without anyone meaning to do so.

Instruction and Accountability Challenges

Educators in reforming schools tend to worry about the threat to creativity posed by new state mandates. One of the schools I studied had had the freedom of choosing its own successful literacy program, but feared that new state tests would not allow them the time to continue in this direction. Control of the agenda had slipped, along with the teachers' control over their preferred method of teaching: cooperative learning and hands-on instruction. As one teacher put it, "It's very hard to do that if you are concerned about every bit of knowledge." Teachers felt that they, their students, and the school would be rewarded or punished for performance on standardized tests regardless of what their professional judgment told them to do.

One 1st grade teacher at the school told me about the demise of an interdisciplinary unit she had developed on worms. Students in this unit had observed worms, read and wrote about them, and even learned how to serve them as food. Because the unit had enjoyed great praise from parents and children, replacing it was hard, but the teacher felt that test preparation must come first. Still, she worried that her students were exchanging engaging instruction and meaningful learning for the anxieties of standardized testing. All she could do was hope that the political winds would change for future 1st graders.

Assessment and Accountability Challenges

Not surprisingly, this was *the* area that drew the most focused concern from teachers and administrators I met. This makes sense since it is from the standardized tests that the state, and now the federal government, will largely make decisions about student, teacher, administrator, school, and district rewards and sanctions. One administrator raised the question of test validity when he wondered whether or not the tests really measured the content that they purported to measure.

A different and equally troubling validity question is that of alignment: In one case, 9th graders were given a social studies test with content questions that they simply had not been exposed to in class. The school's principal saw this as a serious problem and thought that one possible solution, expanding the curriculum to include the test items, was equally problematic. If her school kept on expanding the curriculum to cover test items as well as content that her staff felt was crucial, it would be breaking faith with its mission. Educators at this school worked hard to refine a curriculum that centered less on superficial coverage and more on depth. At another high school, one teacher found that some mandatory standardized tests emphasized what he called "factoids" over concepts. However, he praised other tests that used science laboratories to measure skill development.

Along with this support for authentic assessment was a defense of portfolios. Not all educators resisted standardized tests—many simply wanted the tests aligned to their own curriculum, and the assessment to be comprehensive. Teachers frequently mentioned such familiar concepts as "growth over time" and "multiple snapshots of student development." They feared that their students would be measured unfairly by an expensive and intrusive testing program that could reduce their schools to what one administrator called a "test culture."

Deeper Concerns Over Control from Above

Underlying the curriculum-instruction-assessment particulars are even deeper questions that get to the heart of innovating schools. Educators at these schools feel that their state's accountability systems threaten to distort the very meaning of teaching. They understand the accountability system, but they object to it. One veteran teacher who spent many years helping her school to reform described the accountability system to me this way:

> Part of it is coming from an honorable place. We don't want white middle-class kids taught to one standard and black inner-city kids taught another. So one set of standards means one set of tests— this will raise the bar for everyone, this will be more equitable. Of course, the problem from my point of view as a teacher in this school is that they don't think of the unintended negative effects, and they don't think about the resources necessary to get to that point. There are all these shortcuts you can use to get people through tests that are not good teaching and good learning. We spend so much time thinking of what the standards are going to be, what the tests are going to be, that we don't think of what the implementation issues are.

Teachers and administrators believe that their professional efficacy is challenged by the imposition of accountability systems, which they believe take on a life of their own. Many teachers at reforming schools feel that their judgment, creativity, and hard work are all now called into question. Some of the teachers I spoke with could see that it would be easy to simply give in and withdraw from taking responsibility for the learning program at their schools, but found this unacceptable. To one educator, there was now a contest between teacher empowerment and control from the state.

Yet the demands of the state, and now the federal government, are tied to funding and will not be ignored. Knowing this, teachers and building leaders at the schools I researched lamented the fact that the newly required curriculum revisions would take valuable time away from direct work with students and continued work on curriculum, instruction, and local assessment programs, all of which had yielded impressive results. Such huge shifts in the reform agenda made some wonder whether the testing system was the only reality. If so, was all of their work now somehow unreal? A guidance counselor gave one example showing how bizarre the state testing process could be. A young woman who had been in 12th grade the previous year could not graduate because she had failed one part of her state's reading test by a single question. "She enrolled in college and is already in college-level English classes," said the counselor. "She's beyond the remedial classes at the university. She's taking English 101 and she's passing it. She can't yet pass the high school standardized test so she can't get out of high school but she is already succeeding in college. It shows you how crazy this is."

All of the increased stresses surrounding the accountability system caused several teachers and administrators to predict early retirement for others and consider such options for themselves. This is both understandable and highly regrettable since these are the exact people that our educational system most desperately needs due to their knowledge, creativity, and proven record of achievement in designing new possibilities for our school systems.

Many educators question the factory model that the top-down nature of state mandates represents. As one teacher at a successful innovating school noted, "Are you training kids to work in a factory, or are you training kids to think, analyze, create, go beyond . . . memorization, regurgitation, and repeating?"

The famous education writer John Holt compared this kind of one-size-fits-all mentality to the mythical Procrustes, who would stretch short victims or cut off the legs of tall ones until they fit the length of his bed. If this is a fair criticism, we should wonder how this insistence on uniformity prepares students for an unpredictable world where flexibility, invention, and initiative are required from nearly everyone.

Many in reforming schools feel that there is an anti-innovation bias coming from their state capitals. State accountability systems seem to hit the most creative schools hardest; as one principal told me, "The schools are being handcuffed." Many bemoan state timetables as well—"In education it seems that we rarely give things enough time to work," I was told. Rather than trust educators, many of the educators I spoke with saw outside forces pressing for change before there was time to really test the changes already underway. These pressures were especially hard on veteran staff, many of whom were intrinsically motivated and did not see a coherent vision from their state. Sadly, some of the most gifted people I met in my research wondered whether it was still safe to innovate.

Coping Strategies

In addition to offering serious and thoughtful criticism of the imposed accountability systems in their states, educators at the schools I researched developed a series of attitudes and behaviors for responding effectively. To begin with, they recommended a positive attitude. One teacher wanted to remind his colleagues that during an earlier round of state tests, their school was able to combine creativity with successful results; another felt that they should always remember that their hard work would help to pull them through. These were not failing schools with underperforming students and teachers.

Concrete teacher behaviors were also used by veteran teachers who became models of innovation and test awareness. In this way, teachers felt that they could insulate their students from what one person called "the worst excesses" of the testing process. Besides the common practice of careful curriculum mapping, one high school employed mini-units to cover test items. The benefit of this technique was that the school's own core curriculum would remain intact while specifics from the state test could be taught, albeit in isolation.

Principal leadership also helped the students at reforming schools to do well in tests without giving up on their own development agendas. Principals asked their faculties not to overreact to the new tests and to keep the focus on teaching and learning within the school's mission. This meant the principals needed to take risks in order to make a safe space for their faculty. Remembering earlier days of the reform process, one principal told me:

> Nothing was going to happen if I was not going to protect teachers in the school for their risk-taking. I had to. I could not allow them to be sabotaged from outside this place. This had to be a safe haven for them. When the hits came, I was willing to take it and I saw it as my job.

Such behavior seems especially timely today. Principals in these schools realize that they greatly influence how the agenda is developed and shared, as well as their school's emotional climate. Staying on target, remembering that their first job is effective teaching, reminding teachers that they are already successful and that the school has a powerful mission—all of these things make a difference to teachers. For their part, successful principals know that their schools' shared governance systems are a bedrock of stability during volatile times and support careful curriculum-instruction-assessment analysis at both the building and district levels; by participating enthusiastically and maintaining strong ties to the central office, principals help project their schools' influence on the district leaders.

Action Strategy: The Curriculum-Instruction-Assessment Triangle

As we have already seen in Chapter 8 (Figure 8.1), the curriculum-instruction-assessment triangle is at the core of school reform. By reflecting on this triangle, you can gain a better understanding of your school's unique program and how these elements are alive and subject to change from interior and exterior forces.

Applying the Curriculum-Instruction-Assessment Triangle to Your School

Step 1: Determine Current Conditions.
Begin your reflection by answering the questions in Figure 11.3.

Step 2: Describe Externally Mandated Changes to Curriculum, Instruction, and Assessment. It is crucial that educators not blame the district for the changes it imposes, but carefully analyze differences between your school's learning agenda and the changes being considered. To do this, answer the questions in Figure 11.4.

Step 3: Find Your Place on the ROTIE Continuum. Place your school where you think it best fits on the continuum in Figure 11.5. Repeat, only this time placing your school where you think others in the district would place you. If there are discrepancies between the two placements, you need to engage in deep communication to align perceptions.

Step 4: Consider Your Options. During times of low stress, it may be possible to exist almost anywhere along the ROTIE spectrum without great pressure to change. Indeed, during much of the 1990s schools were asked to experiment with curriculum, instruction, and assessment as part of the restructuring movement. By the end of that decade, however, there were new pressures placed upon districts by most states in the form of standards and high-stakes testing. One consequence is that there is now a great deal of pressure coming from state capitals to school districts to perform well on standardized tests. This has been taken up at the national level in the form of No Child Left Behind legislation, which in turn results in pressure from the central office to schools. In the case of reforming schools, this means pressure to conform to curriculum-instruction-assessment patterns that are not always part of their original mission. So, the first thing for

---

FIGURE 11.3
QUESTIONS FOR REFLECTING ON CURRENT SCHOOL CONDITIONS

Curriculum

What is at the heart of your curriculum? Is there a core curriculum concept?

Are subjects normally tied together in some kind of coherent whole?

Are students' developmental and emotional needs taken into account in the learning agenda?

Does the curriculum include room for arts and athletics?

Who made the decisions that led to your current curriculum? Did teachers, parents, or students have some say? If not, how might that have changed the outcome of your curriculum?

Upon what body of knowledge was your curriculum based? What is the source of its authority?

How flexible has your curriculum been to development over time?

Instruction

Does your school ascribe to a constructivist approach to learning?

In what ways does learning at your school reflect such ideas as Howard Gardner's theory of multiple intelligences? Does your school's approach to instruction include thematic units?

Does team teaching play a part?

How was your school's instructional model developed, and who helped develop it?

Assessment

Do your school's students use projects, portfolios, or demonstrations to show what they have learned?

What role do traditional tests and quizzes play in your school?

How has your school's report card been modified over the years to better align with the learning program?

If you work at a high school, is there a senior exhibition before graduation for students to show how much they've progressed?

How were assessment methods decided at your school? Who was involved, and what did they contribute to the assessment designs?

strategists to evaluate is the degree of local pressure now and in the near future. After that judgment has been made, here are three possible moves to discuss:

Option 1: Ignore the continuum and maintain your current course. The upside: Integrity will be maintained. The downside: You will risk conflict with the central office and the public. The strategy: You will likely need to increase external affiliations and increase your power base to prepare for severe turbulence, and plan to win in the contest of wills between you and the higher authorities.

Option 2: Move strategically to the perceived new boundary. Through careful analysis, you will need to determine how far

---

FIGURE 11.4
QUESTIONS FOR REFLECTING ON THE POTENTIAL EFFECT OF CHANGES TO THE LEARNING AGENDA

Curriculum

What are the priorities of your school's current learning agenda? To what extent are these integrated into the core curriculum?

Where did the mandated changes originate, and how were they developed? What is the source of their authority?

Upon what body of knowledge are the mandated changes based?

How responsive is the current curriculum to changes over time?

Instruction

Is the state or district mandating new instructional processes at your school? If so, how were these changes developed, and upon what knowledge are they based?

Are there any proposed changes to curriculum that might affect the type of instruction your school can provide?

Assessment

Is the state or district mandating new assessment measures at your school? If so, how were these measures developed, and upon what knowledge are they based?

What would success or failure with the new assessments mean to your school?

What do your students and their families know or feel about the assessments?

to the right on the ROTIE scale you'd need to move in order to maintain your mission and remain under the district's umbrella. The upside: Your mission may stay largely intact with no inevitable conflict. The downside: Considerable changes to curriculum, instruction, and assessment are likely if you are to meet state expectations and still maintain your mission; staff tensions will probably rise as a result of changes; changes may still not be sufficient to satisfy the district or the state. The strategy: You will need to carefully map the curriculum-instruction-assessment triangle at your school and increase dialogue with the central office to connect the school's mission to the district's. One argument in your favor is the tradition of local control over educational decisions.

Prepare for moderate to severe turbulence, largely felt inside of the school.

Option 3: Move Well Within the "Essential" Range. Although this may sound like surrender, sometimes a school has no choice but to comply with mandated changes. The upside: Tensions between the school and district will be reduced; goals will be aligned, leading to new resources such as money for professional development in district programs. If you elect to move in this direction, your school may survive to try reforms anew under more favorable circumstances. The downside: Loss of the original mission; a sense of failure. The strategy: You will need to prioritize elements of the original mission in specific curriculum-instruction-

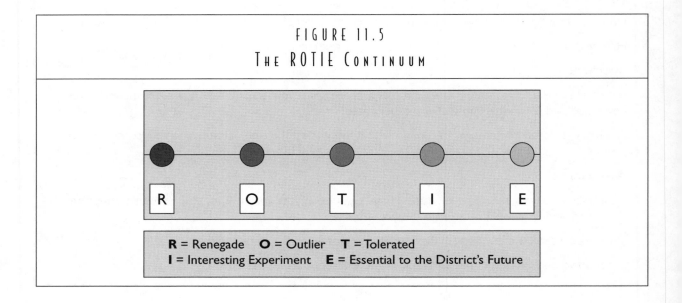

FIGURE 11.5
THE ROTIE CONTINUUM

R   O   T   I   E

R = Renegade   **O** = Outlier   **T** = Tolerated
I = Interesting Experiment   **E** = Essential to the District's Future

assessment terms and keep what can be kept. You may have to negotiate with district and state officials to keep certain elements intact. Because resistance to your original mission may be quite strong in the environment surrounding the school, you will need to be highly flexible. In the meantime, work on the next season of reforms while protecting children from the worst excesses of the mandates. Prepare for severe turbulence among administrators, staff members, teachers, students, and families.

12

Recasting the Vision Without Selling Out
ONE SCHOOL'S STORY

OFTEN THE BEST WAY TO CONVEY AN IMPORTANT POINT IS WITH A COMPELLING true story. For the final chapter of this book, I have decided to take this route. Perhaps your innovation is facing challenges from the district, state, or national levels, and you are perfectly capable of responding to them. I hope that the information found in this chapter will be of use to you and that you may continue in your own reform program, smoothly sailing on.

If, however, you are finding it nearly impossible to continue reforms despite your school's best efforts to engage in turbulence effectively, you may be wondering what your options are. The story of Jacquie Werner-Gavrin and the Red Cedar School will illustrate what I call recasting the vision without selling out.

The Red Cedar School in Bristol, Vermont, was founded in 1989 by Jacquie and two other teachers. After working within the public school system for many years, the teachers had decided to create their own school in order to promote their educational ideas in a freer atmosphere. Their inspiration was the Sudbury Valley School in Framingham, Massachusetts, which was founded on the belief that children have the right to set their own learning directions rather than follow the dictates of adults. As one of that school's leaders wrote:

> The starting point for all of our thinking was the apparently revolutionary idea that a child is a person, worthy of full respect as a human being. These are simple words with devastatingly complex consequences, chief of which

is that the child's agenda for his own life is as important as anyone else's agenda—parents, family, friends, or even the community. (Greenberg & Sadofsky, 1992)

Based on this philosophy, the three teachers opened the Red Cedar School, allowing children to decide what they wanted to learn, when they wanted to learn it, and for how long they wanted to engage in it. In addition, the school did not discriminate between play and academic work, making students responsible for their choices. Community was established through a shared governance system in which students and adults considered the school's needs and how to meet them, including hiring decisions and need for revenue. There was also a student and staff council that established codes of behavior and met with students who violated them.

Clearly, this kind of student-centered, democratic school endeavor was both bold and innovative. It was also remarkably different from any experiment that I had seen. With my curiosity stirred, I asked and was given permission to visit the school. This led to the first of two research projects at the school (Gross, 2001). In the first venture, I interviewed three teenage students who had spent all of their school years at Red Cedar. I wanted to know what kind of activities students would choose for themselves without any outside pressure. Through their reflections I saw a pattern of learning quite unlike anything I had seen in more traditionally organized schools. One girl had started to decode words at about age five. "I had a cup at home that said, 'Milk is good food,' on it and it had a cow on it and 'food' had a lot of 'O's because the cows mooed," she said. "I remember reading it. I remember looking at it, and all of a sudden, I knew how to read. I knew exactly what those words meant. . . . From then on, I just learned how to read everything." Because this girl was a Red Cedar student, she read when she wanted to for as long as she wanted to. In her case, this meant reading nearly every book in the school's library for years at a time. But she also played and made friends, learned about art, and explored mathematics quite regularly.

In their own ways, the other two students had equally impressive experiences to share. I also found that all three students had progressed in nearly every one of Vermont's twenty Vital Results learning categories. Delving further, I conducted a longitudinal study with six Red Cedar students, interviewing them twice a year over two years. Their personal learning odysseys, though unique, underscored the value of this kind of learning environment, at least for certain kinds of students.

Red Cedar continued for a dozen years, developing many fine individual experiences and impressive group programs, such as a traveling choir that specialized in international folk songs. The school's student body population grew to the mid-20s, yet the ideal of growing larger and finding true financial stability seemed elusive, causing serious doubts about the school's long term future. At this point, the school's leaders, students, and families decided to take bold action.

The first phase of action was problem awareness. Jacquie and her colleagues in the school community gathered data carefully to see what their current situation was. They realized that they were drawing students from a fairly rural part of a largely rural state. This made the Red Cedar situation different from the Sudbury Valley School that had been its inspiration. Jacquie wondered with her colleagues whether this area could support a school with such a specific and nontraditional approach. They had made a go of things for this long, but what were their long-term prospects? She also thought about the changing educational environment in the state and in the country. An open feeling of experimentation was now being replaced by greater focus on curriculum standards and assessments. Were the practices of the Red Cedar School important philosophically but unattractive to many families? Was the school too far from the norm that parents wanted for their children?

Next, Jacquie led the school into a period of community outreach and problem-solving. I attended one meeting of parents on a Saturday morning at Red Cedar. Gathered in a tight circle in the sunlit meeting room were about 18 parents, students, and staff members. Each took a turn speaking about the school—its past, present, and possible future. The discussion was aimed at gaining consensus on the need to put Red Cedar on a safer course. At the same time, the group was clear that the school should not turn its back on the principles of democracy and wide student choice. Through meetings such as this, Jacquie found enough direction to move to the next step.

With the help of a smaller group, the reinvention of Red Cedar went into a third phase. Now it was time to consider how to make the school more attractive to more students, while not losing what made it so powerful in its early years. The group studied and asked for advice from many quarters. Many colleagues involved with the Sudbury Valley School model were understanding and supportive, giving the Red Cedar planners a sense of continuity. The group decided that the renewed school would have specific learning outcomes and encourage students in broad but well-defined directions. The feeling of the planning group was that it could accomplish this and still allow for many learning choices for students. This strategy would retain the confidence of the original families that had been loyal to Red Cedar for many years and attract new students from families not comfortable with the school's early approach to education. Allied with this step in the reinvention process was a very careful look at budgeting, marketing, and possible foundation support for the school.

During the spring of 2002, the Red Cedar School did two crucial things at once. It ran a successful semester in the original model, and paved the way for the new version of the school. With continued hard work, a great amount of discussion, and trust in their own ability to invent, the renewed Red Cedar School was successfully launched in September of 2002. With its opening, Jacquie had led an important transition. Her efforts had helped everyone at the school to recast its vision without selling out.

Action Strategy: Dialogue, Democracy, and Innovation

Looking at the Red Cedar story, I wondered what were the underlying qualities that made such an impressive strategic move possible. In this study and in a related one led by a public school principal in the middle of a huge metropolitan community, I found three core principles:

- Dialogue, or a commitment to almost continuous communication by all faculty and administrators;
- Democracy, or the belief in equality and shared power among members of the school's community; and
- Innovation, or the spirit of continuous invention and refinement to further the mission of the school.

These principles do not exist as mere platitudes, but appear to operate together in a dynamic system that is mutually reinforcing, like the curriculum-instruction-assessment triangle. When there is greater authentic dialogue, for instance, more voices are heard on crucial issues and power has a greater chance of being shared (democracy). With more voices focusing on a topic, there is an increased possibility for a novel idea to surface (innovation). Similarly, when democracy is nurtured, more participation is called for, increasing the need for dialogue, possibly leading to new organizational patterns (innovation). If authentic innovation becomes a priority, as opposed to a simple fad, it should be grounded in the deepest need of the school and supported by the work of the faculty and staff. This suggests an emphasis on dialogue (so that needs might surface) and democracy (shared work to nurture, support, and sustain the innovation over time).

But how does this process fit the reinvention of the Red Cedar School? In the first phase of its work, the school's team started a series of expanding discussions and reflections. These were profound dialogues that brought new information to bear and created a sense of common purpose. A constant value in the life of Red Cedar is a foundational faith in democracy, so it is no wonder that the conversations were open, inclusive, and devoid of hierarchy and manipulation. This did not mean that they were aimless—just the opposite: Because the school was facing serious challenges, the democratic dialogues were intense, congenial, and motivating, and led to a phase of innovation whereby the new outlines of the school and the strategies needed to implement the transition emerged.

As the dialogue-democracy-innovation diagram in Figure 12.1 shows, all of these qualities are mutually reinforcing. Dialogue opens up the possibility for serious discussion of deep and troubling issues without surrendering to unwarranted fear. The fact that these dialogues are democratic means that the voices of all stakeholders are heard, and everyone can feel that the process honors their humanity. This leads to the innovation

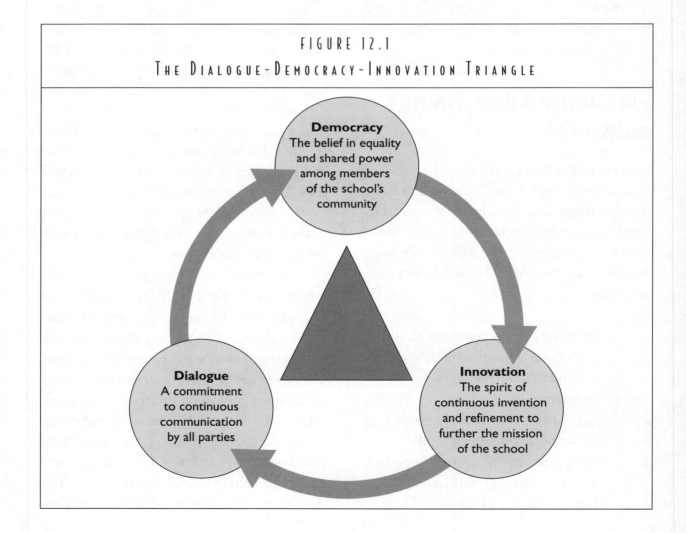

FIGURE 12.1
THE DIALOGUE-DEMOCRACY-INNOVATION TRIANGLE

Democracy
The belief in equality and shared power among members of the school's community

Dialogue
A commitment to continuous communication by all parties

Innovation
The spirit of continuous invention and refinement to further the mission of the school

required to place the school on safer ground for the long term. Again, this innovation is made more creative and more likely to succeed because it stems from the combined wisdom of a dedicated, empowered group.

Applying the Dialogue-Democracy-Innovation Model to Your School

Stage 1: Uncover the Dimensions of the Challenge

To apply the core principles of successful reinvention to your setting, begin by uncovering the dimensions of the challenge at hand. To do this, your planning team should:

- Cut across old boundaries that separate teachers from parents, and students from administrators and staff.
- Conduct numerous small group discussions that give everyone a voice and dignify all contributions.
- Allow time for the process to unfold. Remember, this is neither window dressing nor a departure from real work. When profound change is required, your greatest chance for success is through comprehensive dialogue.

Stage 2: Build a Vision

- Create a feedback loop. Make sure that the dialogues start with a shared, focusing question. Record the responses, inventions, and developments in those discussions and share the combined findings. In qualitative research, this step is known as "member checking." It is your way of assuring accuracy and building a shared vision of realities as well as future possibilities.
- Through feedback loops, find the seeds of new possibilities. Open the discovery process up to everyone. Look broadly at the current forces in your environment and at relevant models beyond your area.
- Explore "what if" possibilities—again, including all school community groups. Here, the democratic process informs your innovation as well as the dialogues needed to nurture it.
- Refine your approach. By now, you will have a clear sense of the issues challenging your school, as well as the kernels of the new form your school might take. You have helped give birth to a new model that fits the challenges of these times *and* keeps faith with your core beliefs.

Stage 3: Prepare for Implementation

The invention process is born of democratic dialogue and innovation. Now all three
parts of the dialogue-democracy-innovation
triangle come into play once more as you move
from plan to action. Just as Red Cedar School
did, you will likely need to test-market, consider budgeting, conduct outreach, and set a
target date for your change process to come
alive. As in the other two stages, you will need
to continue dialogues, maintain a democratic
organization, and commit to constant innovation and adjustment as you carry through to
the first years of your school's new form.

Conclusion to Challenge 4

The process of sustaining reform is both an internal challenge and one of navigating the turbulent waters of the outside world. The innovating school needs to be expert in both of these. When a district experiences changes, there may be extensive alterations to what was once a supportive relationship. Simply put, the new leadership team may not value the reform agenda. Even the same district leadership may be under new pressures and not nearly as responsive to your school's reform program. This is not a time to panic or to lose hope. If your district is hiring a new leader, you need to ensure your school's role in that crucial decision. If circumstances change for the worse, you would be well advised to consider what sources of power you have at your disposal—not to mount a hopeless campaign, but to shore up your program and bring all of your assets together.

When the state and federal governments come into the picture, a similar level of assertive behavior is recommended. First, it is vital that your school's community understand that accountability comes in at least three varieties, not one monolithic form. Second, you may wish to consider the difference between mere accountability and the deeper concept of responsibility. Learning from the shared experiences of the schools in this study, many insights are available to you in the realms of curriculum, instruction, and assessment conditions. By understanding these, you may be able to better protect your own program from unwelcome pressures that threaten to upend your successful work.

In all cases, you should remember to work methodically and strategically, even when you may want to respond emotionally. Often, there will be several options and willing helpers in unexpected places. Finally, if all else fails, there is the option of recasting your vision altogether. The Red Cedar example shows all of us how this can be done with integrity.

Conclusion

The only thing we have to fear is fear itself.

—Franklin D. Roosevelt's First Inaugural Address, March 1933

AT THE BEGINNING OF THIS BOOK, I POSED FOUR CHALLENGING QUESTIONS:

1. How can reforming schools face leadership succession effectively?
2. How can they keep their learning agenda alive?
3. How can the culture of reform be sustained over time?
4. How can schools face the turbulence of new district, state, and national demands?

Facing Leadership Succession

Saying goodbye to a strong, visionary principal can be emotional for students, teachers, and parents. The principals at the schools I visited had an impressive blend of professional skills, strong intuitive powers, and immense dedication to their schools. Their work and strategic prowess helped start reforms and led to many triumphs along the way. The effect of their efforts on student achievement was quite clear, making their departures all the more difficult.

The findings presented in this book show that schools should select the types of leaders that best fit their own stage of development: For example, a school in the middle of an important development should probably not choose a leader who has a very different direction in mind, whereas schools with mature reform agendas that need new challenges might want precisely such a principal. Once hired, principals can benefit greatly from a comprehensive mentoring program that ensures they don't have to face their new jobs in isolation. If a school has trouble finding an appropriate principal to hire, one alternative is to create a teacher leadership team along the lines of the one used by Otter Valley Union High School.

Keeping the Learning Agenda Alive

At the start of the reform process, there is normally a burst of energy and enthusiasm during which teachers, administrators, and parents collaborate on curriculum building and designing new learning experiences. Ironically, the very success of these efforts can lead to additional stress for the school in the form of overly rapid growth and rising expectations. The district view is too often that if a school is doing well with a few students, it can easily do just as well with many more. Negative and positive feedback loops and single and double looping can help educators deflect such unwarranted pressure—particularly since almost all innovating schools employ shared governance structures.

Sustaining the Culture of Reform

We know that schools become a world unto themselves with their own culture. This is especially true of innovative schools where professional life is intense and everyone seems interconnected. But all schools have very porous boundaries. New teachers enter the system regularly. New students and their families are a constant part of school life. How can a culture be sustained with so many changes? The wisdom of the schools in this study teaches us that there are ways to bring new people into the reforming school very successfully. At the center of these techniques is the belief that this is a two-way street. These schools are designed to respond to new people in two ways. First, there is a great deal of listening and responding to the new person, whether she is a faculty member or a student. The school really belongs to the community and it needs to change with every new citizen. Second, there are flexible and interactive ways for newcomers to learn about the school they have joined. What is striking about these schools is that they balance the task of welcoming new people with the equally crucial job of sustaining advanced teacher-learners. These teachers are treated with great respect and given serious leadership responsibilities. They are also supported in their own professional development as experts.

Navigating an Honorable Course through District, State, and National Upheavals

Along with internal turbulence, reforming schools often face district, state, and national pressures. These pressures can strike at the heart of their curriculum-instruction-assessment program and threaten years of work. I do not believe that this is inevitable. Understanding the meaning of leadership changes at the district level is essential for school leaders who wish their reform programs to continue. District leaders are themselves facing great pressures that can easily be directed down to the schools in an era of high-stakes testing and accountability. The No Child Left Behind legislation takes accountability up a huge notch by nationalizing the issue. Clearly understanding the differences between the curriculum-instruction-assessment of the state and that of the school seems to be a practical first step for innovating schools. Considering where that places the school is a logical follow-up. Turbulence may be unavoidable but that does not mean it needs to overwhelm the school. A thoughtful captain may need to steer through some rough water on the way to shore, but she does not have to aim for the middle of the worst of it. In fact, turbulence is a normal part of the movement of boats *and* schools. It gives the energy to consider change in the first place and to move away from comfortable old habits. The wise leader and leadership team can distinguish between the type of turbulence that gives the needed spark and that which is only destructive. Facing only a tidal wave, the thoughtful leader should reflect on the decisions made at the Red Cedar School. It is possible to recast the vision without selling out your school's values.

Conclusion

I am always impressed with how complex a job it is to initiate and sustain the work of school innovation. Looking at the problems described in this book, it easily could be considered daunting. However, I believe that the true message from these schools is one of hope and an appeal to our courage and optimism. It reminds me of Franklin D. Roosevelt's first inaugural address. For our nation, March 1933 was a time of financial panic. On the very morning of the inauguration, outgoing President Hoover claimed that his administration was "at the end of [its] rope." Roosevelt reversed this mood starting with his first speech.

For those of us who support inventive, creative, student-centered schools, this may also be a time of panic and depression. So this paraphrase of Roosevelt's inaugural may indeed be a fitting message. I imagine a figure, strong and confident, looking out at a throng of hopeful educators:

This is preeminently the time to speak the truth, the whole truth, frankly and boldly. We need not shrink from honestly facing conditions in our country today. This great spirit of educational innovation will endure as it has endured, will revive, and will prosper. So first of all let me assert my firm belief that the only thing we need to fear is fear itself— nameless, unreasoning, unjustified terror that paralyzes needed efforts to convert retreat into advance.

Being an innovating school is rewarding but rarely easy, especially in this era of severe and even extreme turbulence. One of the hardest feelings that educators have is the sense that they are alone in their journey on a vast sea in a small craft. I hope that the story of initiating innovation that I introduced in *Staying Centered*, and have continued in *Promises Kept,* has helped you to see that you are hardly alone. It is a difficult passage, but you are part of a great fleet of schools all across the world who are striving to reach a better place for students and the community. Sustaining yourself and your school takes strategy, collaboration, and planning. If this book has given you some pointers for your voyage, it has served its purpose. This is certainly an adventure, and one that is necessary if we are serious about enriching and sharing a democratic vision for our world.

References

Anderson, S., Rolheiser, C., & Gordon, K. (1998). In Ontario: Preparing teachers to be leaders. *Educational Leadership, 55*(2), 559–561.

Bank Street College. (1992). *The Principals' Institute 1990–1992.* New York: New York City Board of Education.

Bateson, M. C. (1989). *Composing a life.* New York: Grove Atlantic.

Beck, L., & Murphy, J. (1995). *School-based management as school reform.* Thousand Oaks, CA: Corwin Press.

Bolman, L., & Deal, T. (1993). *The path to school leadership: A portable mentor.* Thousand Oaks, CA: Corwin Press.

Boon, S. L. Z. (1998). Principalship mentoring in Singapore: Who and what benefits? *Journal of School Administration, 36*(1), 29–43.

Bruner, J., Goodnow, J., & Austin, A. (1956). *A study of thinking.* New York: Wiley.

Burns, J. M. (1978). *Leadership.* New York: Harper Colophon.

Calabrese, R. L., & Tucker-Ladd, P. R. (1991). The principal and assistant principal: A mentoring relationship. *NASSP Bulletin, 75,* 67–74.

Calahan, H. A. (1932/1999). *Learning to sail.* Mineola, NY: Dover Publications.

Cohn, K. C., & Sweeny, R. C. (1992). *Principal mentoring programs: Are school districts providing the leadership?* Paper presented at a meeting of the American Educational Research Association, San Francisco. (ERIC Document Reproduction Service No. ED 345 376)

Coleman, M. M., Low, G. T., Bush, T., & Chew, O. A. J. (1996). *Re-thinking training for principals: The role of mentoring.* Paper presented at a meeting of the American Educational Research Association, New York. (ERIC Document Reproduction Service No. ED 397 479)

Cooley, V., & Shen, J. (1999). Who will lead? The top ten factors that influence teachers moving into administration. *NASSP Bulletin, 83,* 75–80.

Creighton, T. (1997). *Teachers as leaders: Is the principal really needed?* Eugene, OR: Clearinghouse for Educational Management.

Crow, G. M., & Matthews, L. J. (1998). *Finding one's way: How mentoring can lead to dynamic partnership.* Thousand Oaks, CA: Corwin Press.

Daresh, J., & Playko, M. (1993). *Benefits of a mentoring program for aspiring administrators.* Paper presented at a meeting of the American Association of School Administrators, Orlando, Florida. (ERIC Document Reproduction Service No. ED 354 603)

Dewey, J. (1903). *Democracy and education.* New York: The Free Press.

Erasmus, M., & van der Westhuizen, P. C. (1994). *Guidelines for the professional development of school principals by means of a mentoring system in a developing country.* Paper presented at the International Intervisitation Programme, Buffalo, New York. (ERIC Document Reproduction Service No. ED 371 440)

Erikson, E. (1980). *Identity and the life cycle* (2nd ed.). New York: Norton.

Fullan, M. G., & Stiegerbauer, S. (1991). *The new meaning of educational change.* New York: Teachers College Press.

Georgia Department of Education. (1990). *Teacher support specialist guide and resource manual.* Atlanta: Author.

Gordon, G. E., & Rosen, R. (1981). Critical factors in leadership succession. *Behavior and Human Performance, 27,* 227–254.

Greenberg, D., & Sadofsky, M. (1992). *The Sudbury Valley experience.* Framingham, MA: Sudbury Valley Press.

Gross, S. J. (1998). *Staying centered: Curriculum leadership in a turbulent era.* Alexandria, VA: Association for Supervision and Curriculum Development.

Gross, S. J. (1999). *Life after Moses: The fate of selected innovative institutions beyond the transformational leader.* Paper presented at a meeting of the American Educational Research Association, Montreal, Québec.

Gross, S. J. (2001). Crafting one's own curriculum: The story of students who design their own learning agendas. *The Journal for Critical Inquiry in Curriculum and Instruction, 2,* 38–44.

Gross, S. J., Shaw, K. M., & Shapiro, J. P. (2002). Deconstructing accountability through the lens of democratic philosophies: Toward a new analytic framework. *Journal of Research for Educational Leaders, 1*(3), 5-27.

Grusky, O. (1960). *Administrative theory in transition.* Victoria, Australia: Deakin University Press.

Gunter, M. A., Estes, T. H., & Schwab, J. (1999). *Instruction: A models approach* (3rd ed.). Boston: Allyn and Bacon.

Hart, A. W. (1985). *Succession as social validation: The view from inside the principalship.* Paper presented at a meeting of the American Educational Research Association, Chicago.

Hoy, W., & Aho, F. (1973). Patterns of succession in high school principals and organizational change. *Planning and Change, 4*(2), 82–88.

Koopman, O., Miel, A., & Misner, P. (1943). *Democracy in school administration.* New York: Appleton-Century.

Kuhn, T. (1962). *The structure of scientific revolutions.* Chicago: The University of Chicago Press.

Lambert, L., Collay, M., Dietz, M., & Kent, K. (1997). *Who will save our schools? Teachers as constructivist leaders.* Thousand Oaks, CA: Corwin Press.

Lao-Tse. (1988). *Tao Te Ching* (S. Mitchell, Trans.). New York: Harper-Collins.

Lieberman, A. (1995). *The work of restructuring schools.* New York: Teachers College Press.

Lieberman, A., Falk, B., & Alexander, L. (1994). *A culture in the making: Leadership in learner-centered schools.* New York: National Center for Restructuring Education, School, and Teaching.

Leithwood, K. A. (1992). The move toward transformational leadership. *Educational Leadership, 49*(5), 8–12.

Macmillan, R. (1993). *Approaches to leadership succession: What comes with experience?* Paper presented at the Canadian Society for the Study of Education, Ottawa, Ontario.

Mathis, W. (1990). The history of restructuring. *Ventures in Learning, 1,* 1.

Matters, P. (1994). *Mentoring partnerships: Key to leadership success for principals and managers.* Paper presented at a meeting of the International Congress for School Effectiveness and Improvement, Melbourne, Australia. (ERIC Document Reproduction Service No. ED 366 113)

Miskel, C., & Cosgrove, D. (1985). Leadership succession in school settings. *Review of Education Research, 55*(1), 87–105.

Mooney, T. (1994). *Teachers as leaders: Hope for the future.* (ERIC Document Reproduction Service No. ED 380 407)

Morgan, G. (1997). *Images of organization.* Thousand Oaks, CA: Sage Publications.

Nehru, J. (1948/1973). A glory has departed. In L. Copeland & L. Lamm (Eds.), *The world's great speeches.* Mineola, NY: Dover Publications. (Original work presented 1948)

Packard, R., Bas-Isaac, E. (1988). *Educational change and reform: An integrated model for the professional development of teacher leaders.* (ERIC Document Reproduction Service No. ED 302 531)

Paine, T. (1960). *The crisis.* Garden City, NY: Dolphin Books.

Paskey, R. J. (1989). The principal as mentor, partner of assistant principals. *NASSP Bulletin, 73,* 95–98.

Pavan, B. (1986). *Mentors and mentoring functions perceived as helpful to certified aspiring and incumbent female and male public school administrators.* Paper presented at a meeting of the American Educational Research Association, San Francisco. (ERIC Document Reproduction Service No. ED 269 884)

Peel, H. A., Wallace, C., Buckner, K. G., Wrenn, S. L., & Evans, R. (1998). Improving leadership preparation programs through a school, university, and professional organization partnership. *NASSP Bulletin, 82,* 26–34.

Piaget, J. (1952). *The origins of intelligence in children.* New York: Basic Books.

Roberts, J., & Wright, L. V. (1989). *A study of the change efforts among first-time high school principals.* Paper presented at a meeting of the American Educational Research Association, San Francisco. (ERIC Document Reproduction Service No. ED 310 527)

Roosevelt, F. D. (1933/1973). First inaugural address. In L. Copeland & L. Lamm (Eds.), *The world's great speeches.* Mineola, NY: Dover Publications. (Original work presented 1933)

Senge, P. M. (1990). *The fifth discipline.* New York: Doubleday/Currency.

Sergiovanni, T. (1996). *Leadership for the schoolhouse.* San Francisco: Jossey-Bass.

Shapiro, J. P., & Stefkovich, J. A. (2001). *Ethical leadership and decision making in education: Applying theoretical prescriptions to complex dilemmas.* Mahwah, NJ: Lawrence Erlbaum Associates.

Southworth, G. (1995). Reflections on mentoring for new school leaders. *Journal of Educational Administration, 33,* 17–28.

Urbanski, A., & Nickolaou, M. (1997). Reflections on teachers as leaders. *Educational Policy, 11*(2), 243–254.

Vygotsky, L. S. (1978). *Mind in society.* Cambridge, MA: Harvard University Press.

Webb, L., & McCarthy, M. C. (1998). Ella Flagg Young: Pioneer of democratic school administration. *Educational Administration Quarterly, 34*(2), 223–242.

Index

Note: Page numbers followed by the letter *f* indicate figures.

About the Author

STEVEN JAY GROSS IS ASSOCIATE PROFESSOR OF EDUCATIONAL ADMINISTRA-tion at Temple University in Philadelphia and a Senior Fellow at the Vermont Society for the Study of Education. He has also served as Editor of the *ASCD Curriculum Handbook*, Associate Professor of Education at Trinity College of Vermont, Chief of Curriculum and Instruction for the State of Vermont, Executive Director of the China Project Consortium, Curriculum and Staff Development Director for the Rutland Northeast Supervisory Union, and a high school social studies teacher in Philadelphia.

Gross earned his B.A. in history at Temple University, his M.A. in modern Chinese history at the University of Wisconsin, Madison, and his Ed.D. at the University of Pennsylvania. He was also a Klingenstien Fellow at Teachers College, Columbia University. Gross also studied Mandarin Chinese at the Chinese University of Hong Kong.

Gross's first ASCD book was *Staying Centered: Curriculum Leadership in a Turbulent Era* (1998). His research and writing focus on Turbulence Theory and initiating and sustaining deep reform in schools and other educating organizations. He has made numerous presentations and consultations in the United States and abroad, and has published in journals for practitioners, scholars, and the general public.

Despite the commute, the author still lives in Vermont with his family, including Victoria the cat.

Related ASCD Resources

At the time of publication, the following ASCD resources were available; for the most up-to-date information about ASCD resources, go to www.ascd.org. ASCD stock numbers are noted in parentheses.

Audio

Beyond Induction: Become Passionate About Improving Professional Practice by Audrey Lakin (Audiotape # 203211; CD #503304)

Bold Leadership: The Rocky Path to Excellence by Pam Robbins and Harvey Alvy (Audiotape #202160)

Developing Mentoring Programs for Professional Excellence by Pam Robbins (Audiotape #203082)

Leading and Building Community in the Swampy Lowlands of No Easy Answers by Robert Bastress, Betty Collins, Gail Covington McBride, and Eric Mills (CD # 504310)

Multimedia

Educational Leadership on CD-ROM, 1992-98 (#598223)

Creating the Capacity for Change by Jody Mason Westbrook and Valarie Spiser-Albert (#702118)

Guide for Instructional Leaders, Guide 1: An ASCD Action Tool by Roland Barth, Bobb Darnell, Laura Lipton, and Bruce Wellman (#702110)

Books

The Hero's Journey: How Educators Can Transform Schools and Improve Learning by John L. Brown and Cerylle A. Moffett (#199002)

Lessons from Exceptional School Leaders by Mark F. Goldberg (#101229)

1997 ASCD Yearbook: Rethinking Educational Change with Heart and Mind edited by Andy Hargreaves (#197000)

Staying Centered: Curriculum Leadership In a Turbulent Era by Steven Jay Gross (#198008)

Networks

Visit the ASCD Web site (www.ascd.org) and search for "networks" for information about professional educators who have formed groups in the categories of "Instructional Supervision" and "Performance Assessment for Leadership." Look in the "Network Directory" for current facilitators' addresses and phone numbers.

For more information, visit us on the World Wide Web (http://www.ascd.org), send an e-mail message to member@ascd.org, call the ASCD Service Center (1-800-933-ASCD or 703-578-9600, then press 2), send a fax to 703-575-5400, or write to Information Services, ASCD, 1703 N. Beauregard St., Alexandria, VA 22311-1714 USA.